C000101673

Crannóg 58 spring 2023

ISSN 1649-4865
ISBN 978-1-907017-65-0

Cover image: *Red Forest*, by Jean Rooney
Cover image sourced by Sandra Bunting
Cover design by Wordsonthestreet
Published by Wordsonthestreet for Crannóg magazine @CrannogM
www.wordsonthestreet.com @wordsstreet

the arts council
chomhairle ealaíon
funding literature
artscouncil.ie

Comhairle Cathrach na Gaillimhe
Galway City Council

CONTENTS

End of the World
Landa Wo 6
Like a Hook
Shauna Gilligan 7
Song of a Girl Who Would Live as the Fonz
Deborah Bacharach... 12
John Clare's Cremona Violin
Byron Beynon... 13
Dear Daedalus
Annette C. Boehm 14
Ragworm
Phil Cummins.. 15
Campsie Fells, 14th December
Morag Smith... 20
Nature is a Haunted House
Siobhan Campbell 21
Second Sleep
Enda Coyle-Greene 22
The Last Cuppa
Emily Cullen 23
The Bind
David Butler 24
You Can't Go Back
Barbara De Franceschi....................................... 29
Coffee Morning, Herbert Park
Maurice Devitt.. 30
Constellations
Clive Donovan 31
Through The Window A Magpie
Lisa Frank... 32
Swearing Stone
Billy Fenton 38
The Day the Satellites Went Down
Cian Ferriter... 39
Pleasure
Joel Fishbane 40
Mycelium
Bernadette Gallagher 42
Natives
Kevin Graham 43
The Writing of a Letter in a Hostel in a Mountain Pass at Night
Richard W. Halperin.. 44
Career Path
Joanne Hayden 45
Grandmother Spider
Ann Howells.. 50
Calvary
Stephen Shields.. 52

The Nearly New Shop
Laura Treacy Bentley 53
The Dry Dianthus
Jean Tuomey 54
Parsnip Soup
Ana Reisens 55
Archive of an Artist
Maria Isakova Bennett 56
Kiki
Monica Igoe 58
Encounter
Brian Kirk 63
A Week Before the End the Swans Arrive
Sonya MacDonald 64
Trampoline
James Martyn Joyce 65
The New Actaeon
Libby Maxey 71
Storm
Kathy Miles 72
Up the Glen
Deborah Moffatt 74
The Day Philip Larkin Died
Patrick Moran 75
A Home Possessed
Jennifer McMahon 76
Mirror
Jan Mordenski 81
City in October in the Rain
Luke Power 82
Returning to the Garden
Charles Wilkinson 84
Migrations
Susan Isla Tepper 86
The Crannóg Questionnaire
Ron D'Alena 89
Artist's Statement
Jean Rooney 96

Biographical Details 97

Submissions for Crannóg 59 open May 1st until May 31st
Publication date is September 29th 2023

Crannóg is published bi-annually in spring and autumn.

Submission Times:
Month of November for spring issue.
Month of May for autumn issue.

We will <u>not read</u> submissions sent outside these times.

POETRY:
Send no more than three poems. Each poem should be under 50 lines.
PROSE:
Send one story. Stories should be under 2,000 words.

We do not accept postal submissions.
When emailing your submission we require three things:
1. *The text of your submission as a Word attachment.*
2. *A brief bio in the third person.*
3. *A postal address for contributor's copy in the event of publication.*

For full submission details, to learn more about Crannóg magazine,
to purchase copies of the current issue or take out a subscription,
log on to our website:

www.crannogmagazine.com

This issue is dedicated to the memory of

Kevin Higgins

who passed away in January 2023

Sympathy for the Leaves

Praise the thick roots of the tree:
who you are,
who you were,
who you will be.
That which you never see
and often forget,
rough days, keeps you standing here.
For not everything is planted
in the stone flecked earth
you stand in.

Pity the leaves,
those who know not
what throws them about
and out of the garden.
Their whispers
are not opinions
but what way the wind
is sending them just now.

Kevin Higgins, *Crannóg 57*

End of the World

Landa Wo

The three beasts pounced onto the day.
The first sank its fangs into the hours.
The second barked till the end of day.

The third pressed on the button.
The man pushed the limit of the next day.
The day's eyelid closed again
The world ceased to exist.

Kneeling in the ashes and the night
The poet brings together these deformed lines
To build a new reality.

Like a Hook

Shauna Gilligan

KEVIN LIES ON THE SOFA, snoozing after making several false starts on a painting called *forest*. I climb onto him and hang over his mouth like a hook, wishing we were out of sight of those children, hovering, making all that useless noise.

He places his hand over my mouth. 'Shh. Something's happening in our cold seas.'

I shiver, think of the fish we might have had for lunch. *Keep the steamer ready on the flame* was what the recipe had said. *Your peppers will roast gloriously*. I took care with the peppers, ensuring they were sliced perfectly. I diced the onions evenly. But I forgot to keep the steamer ready on the flame.

'But the heat is still there.' I keep my voice low.

But Kevin wiggles from under me. He stands up and brushes down his mustard cord trousers. He glances at the blue velvet sofa and I see what his painter's eyes see, the beautiful contrast.

'Nancy. Now's not the time.' He rubs his eyes with his fists.

'But there's never a time.'

'Snapping at me won't make me change my mind.'

'I'm not getting you to change your mind, I'm just telling you the way it is.'

Kevin pinches his nose with his fat fingers and their still-bitten nails, stained with vermilion. He bites his lower lip, shakes his head. 'Can't you see I'm under enough pressure ...' He takes a deep breath, ends on a question. '... enough pressure?'

This man is so full of images that need to be changed, turned, and even nurtured that he can't finish his sentences. I roll off the sofa and onto the living room floor with a plop.

'Get a hold of yourself.' Spittle flies from Kevin's mouth but I hear the crack in his voice.

Then he leaves the room, quietly. From the scratched wooden floor, I watch his feet retreat, spot specks of dried mud stuck in between the patterns and shapes on his soles. A perfectly formed *L* falls from the left shoe. As always, he'll go talk to the fish in the tank that sits on the kitchen worktop. They'll bob and stare at him with their myopic eyes, transparent and filled with understanding. I wish he'd slammed the door. The wounded one, I'd have been able to shout that he was acting like a child.

I haul myself up and sit against the sofa. I feel the rattle in my chest as I try not to cry. I turn my gaze to the window and the street. Nobody passes. The way it really is, I say to the sofa, the old out-of-tune piano and our empty fireplace, is that the children are not in school. There's not even a baby in a cot, sleeping, in this house.

There are no children.

Those who visit look in our windows, or shout from their overgrown gardens, taunting. The awful quietness of anticipation sits with me. I stare out at half-built shells of houses opposite us, the sky still above them, the evening sun beginning to set. I hear them before I see them.

'Mama Daly, Mama Daly ...'

They are there in a row: five smiling faces propped up on the window ledge by their lean elbows and skinny arms; noses and mouths pressed to the glass. Momentarily they're hidden behind the fog of their breath.

'Mama Daly, Mama Daly ...'

They don't mean anything by this calling, they believe they're playing a game; they might even be of the opinion that they are entertaining. Perhaps they are, I think, our only entertainment. I wave at them and stand up. I go to the hall where I keep a basket of mini chocolate bars. Hidden within this mound of tiny thrills are a couple of full-sized bars.

I open the door, wait for the excited screams, the scuttle of feet. Beyond the children, beyond the unfinished houses, bare, barren fields stretch unendingly. Beyond the horizon seagulls swoop and dive and cry out loudly. I hold out the basket. Each child is allowed one fistful of thrills.

The children, barefoot in their summer clothes, jostle on the doorstep, grabbing handfuls with greedy fists. This evening the girl with the knotted dirty-blonde hair gets a full-sized Kit Kat. She screams and holds it up for the others to see before racing off. I watch her run up the street shouting 'Mama Daly is a god', the others, all four of them after her, filling this neighbourhood with life. If there were dust on the road it would be flying behind those bare legs. I quietly close the front door; I am warm, content. Kevin is behind me. He always stays close when I open the door to our house. He cannot rid himself of the fear of intrusion, of unexpected occurrences.

I turn to him and smile. 'Happiness,' I say, 'is in a full-sized Kit Kat.'

'You shouldn't spoil them like that, you'll never get rid of them.'

I shake my head, hear the rattle in my chest as I try not to cry; those dirty, wild children are what make me a mother.

'And why do you let them call you Mama Daly?'

I don't answer, but walk past him, down the hallway that is wide enough for us to walk side-by-side. The walls are littered with Kevin's images of children looking in windows, sitting on walls, wanting to be seen. In every painting their faces are streaked with dirt. I run my hand over my favourite – the child with the knotted dirty-blonde hair, the girl with her nose squashed against the glass – and press my face to the canvas, sniff the bumps and depths of the oil, long dried. And then I remember David Daly.

*

At eleven I was a flower girl at the wedding of my cousin Sheila and David Daly. My dress was pale green with frills on the bottom and ribbons tightly tied around my waist that sparkled magic in the light. My dress matched Sheila's bouquet: pink roses surrounded by long green leaves of various shades.

'Oh, would you look at her.'

'Cute as a button.'

'She's a dote holding the shining forever-rings.'

All of it was true. I, Nancy, was still cute, small, still, and a dote. I held that forest green velvet cushion out in front of me like it was a bomb. I did not look left or right – as instructed – and the smile on my face did not waiver as I came closer to the backs of Sheila and David. As I reached them, they turned, and I was in awe of them, so perfectly in love. Sheila's smile and David's nod told the world that I was all grown up; I was useful. As they exchanged vows I wondered if there was such a thing as too much happiness. People can die from being too sad and too happy, that's what Sheila had said when I found her weeping on our bathroom floor. Her mother whispered with my mother at the bottom of the stairs; hot tea clutched in their hands.

'Happiness and sadness are the same coin, kid,' Sheila said, waving a little stick at me. 'They are two sides of the same bloody coin.'

'Don't cry,' I said to her.

'You can die,' she said, between breaths of icy air – we still didn't have a radiator in the bathroom – 'you know you can die from happiness.'

She didn't wipe the tears on her cheeks, and shouted *fuck it*, when she threw the stick into the peach bin which, according to my mother, was a perfect match for the bathroom suite. Sheila tried to stand up and couldn't. She started laughing, loudly. I leaned over her to help her. She shook her head and laughed some more.

'Jesus Christ,' she said, 'I'm heavy enough already, what'll I be like in the summer?'

'You'll be happy,' I told her, standing back, giving her room, 'you'll be happy because that's when the sun comes out.' David Daly had told me I had a smile like the sun.

Sheila finally stood up, turned to face me. 'You, sweet girl, will go far!'

'Go far to where?'

But she didn't answer, she just ruffled my hair and I stood, listening to the thud of her feet as she went downstairs.

And at the wedding when David kissed Sheila and everyone clapped, I wondered if anybody else knew that Sheila wasn't the only girl he'd kissed that way.

*

In the kitchen Kevin stands at the table, making shapes with green paint on a white canvas. The light from the floor-to-ceiling windows casts a shadow across his face.

Keep the steamer ready on the flame is what the recipe says. I fill the pot with water, light the gas, set the pot on the heat. I place the steamer on top.

Kevin comes to me, slides his stained hands around my waist and rests them, clasped, on my belly. 'What are you making?'

I watch the steam rise from the bamboo, listen to the quiet trembling of the water as it heats. I turn my head to face him. 'I don't know, yet,' I say.

He kisses my neck. 'I am trying.'

I nod and let him lead me to the window where the silence that stretches between us is long and lovely. In the far distance, beyond the wasteland of unfinished houses, sand dunes wait to be filled, like canvas. I glance over at the fish in the tank, large orange commas swimming in circles, moving through silence. I release myself from the warm hands of Kevin. He returns to his paints, and I go to the worktop and peel a large Spanish onion.

'Shh. Listen.'

I finish peeling the tea-brown skin away, hold the cold layered globe in my hand, and look to where he's pointing. I wipe the tears from my eyes. A bird calls in the stark orange sky; clear, like a bell, sweet like a song and then gone. Something black goes past the window. It's fast and moves higher and out of sight, perhaps over the roof, beyond our house. Something hits the window with a thud. Without saying a word, Kevin drops the tube of grass-green paint and rushes outside.

He returns and stands at the open door holding a plump fish by the tail. Green has covered the vermilion on his fingers and out of the dark fleshy skin of the fish, rainbows blink. I stare and stare, willing the fish to move. The iridescent, lifeless, hook-shaped fish slowly drips onto the clean, tiled floor.

I know there can be no quality in the ingredients if the person producing them is not of quality. So, I look at this man who has asked me so many times to marry him, this man who waits for my acceptance while I wait for my belly to grow so that I can give him a yes.

'Can you believe this?'

I turn from his flushed face to the now dark sky. Will any more shining fish appear? I breathe in the reek – Kevin and the fish – for they are indistinguishable now – and decide that, yes, I believe. I believe in the glorious thing they call love.

The steamer is ready on the flame.

Song of a Girl Who Would Live as the Fonz

Deborah Bacharach

Not for the snap of his fingers,
not for the double thumbs up aaaaay, but for cool
fierceness that leaps from the screen
as I lean in.

If only I could shimmy into black leather!
If only I could throw my arms as wide as a daydream!
If only, most wondrous of all, rev my engine
and be the incantatory growl.

Or I could find myself in front of the band
at the all night dance marathon. For the squats of my Slavic ancestors,
I would, like Fonzie in his bad boy blue jeans,
surrender no grit, suppress no joy.

What are those footsteps?
The rules of a school night?

No, no, it is a warrior with a reed basket
she wove herself, the twelve dancing princesses,
the bard who sings truth to the king.
The room grows crowded.
Make room. Make room.

John Clare's Cremona Violin

Byron Beynon

He held a wedding gift
from Hessey his London publisher
in his Helpstone hands.
The landscape's minutiae
he knew and loved,
it listened for the beating of his heart
true to the countryside's inhabitants,
owl, hedge-sparrow, wren,
the flight of insects,
field-cricket, fox, the ancient badger
that sensed the sounds and rhythms
he'd observed.
When Clare played his violin
on a Northamptonshire night,
the bar was full of promises,
boasts oozed through cracks.
Turning for a moment
he closed his eyes,
concentrated on a note
which circled everyday lives,
waited patiently for
the urgent tempo of the dawn light.

Dear Daedalus

Annette C. Boehm

Your name, I learned today, means 'skillful'.
It is October 1st, and I've painted my nails black.
The summer is gone. Those days of white heat
from above. This summer, again, I did not build
wings. I did not gather all those feathers
strewn in my path. I did nothing for the world
to see. It is October 1st and I've painted
my sails black. The rigging is strong, standing:
shrouds and stays, running: braces and sheets.
This tension holds me – may my raw hands
outlast this season's storms. It is October 1st
and I'm prepared to face the dark outside
with my own dark. I have no wings. But I
have breath and spite. The sun is gone –
it cannot hurt us now. Come, let us fly.

Ragworm

Phil Cummins

GLIDING LIKE A GREAT MILLIPEDE through the oozing mud of the estuary beneath the mussel beds, the ragworm scavenges all in its path. There's the Common Red or Harbour ragworm, sometimes referred to by local fisherman as 'Maddies'. Then there are the Herringbone and White varieties with their unique colourations. But top of the pile is the King rag, a dark devilish-looking hoor of a thing that can grow to nearly a foot in length and sports an evil-looking pair of black pincers, the bane of many a poor angler's fingers. A much-favoured fishing bait, it's been said that the ragworm can tempt virtually anything that swims in the sea by continuing, as it does, to wriggle and writhe long after being skewered on the hook, attempting to squirm to freedom.

We made our way, Gilly and I, along the Coast Road at low tide, my father's garden fork tied up along the Raleigh crossbar with a few lengths of frayed twine. Gilly rode ahead of me pedalling like a dervish, the bucket dangling off the handlebars of his Chopper. Once or twice he instinctively swivelled his curly ginger head leftwards to hoick out a big snotty gullier off the unlucky back window of a parked BMW or Audi. 'POSHY BASTARD!' he howled. That was Gilly, my best mate, hard-wired for wildness.

We stowed the bikes and took a quick slash against the seafront wall.

'We'll be rollin' in dosh,' said Gilly. 'They're shellin' out forty pound a thousand for the rag in town. Sure, we'll have that many picked in a couple of hours. That's a fuckin' score each, man.'

He described in detail how he intended to put his half of the money towards another tattoo, one to match the Grim Reaper he'd already gotten on his right shoulder; a raven perhaps, or maybe even a grinning skull.

'Would you not think of gettin' one as well?' he asked. 'They're deadly.'

'You must be joking,' I replied. 'Those things don't wash off.'

'The birds do go mad for the tats,' he went on. 'They'll get their diddies out for you at the first sight of them.'

'Stop talking shite,' I said, privately wondering if this was actually true. 'Does your aul' fella know you got that done? He'll hop off you when he finds out.'

Gilly shook his head as he zipped his lad up. 'Not yet. Anyway, I'm sixteen. I can do whatever the hell I like. Not as if he's ever going to be sober enough to care one way or another anyway.'

Hefting the bucket and fork, we trudged silently out to the distant mussel beds, shells crunching beneath our wellies as gulls and terns banked and screeched overhead. A light breeze whipped up the sulphury smells of bladderwrack and algae as the late afternoon ferry bound for Holyhead drifted across the horizon. A tennis ball came scooting past us followed by a dripping golden labrador in hot pursuit, it's anorak-wearing owner whistling after it in the distance.

I took up the fork and set to work, each forkful of wet sandy mud seeming to weigh a ton as I grunted with the effort of turning it over to expose the squirming treasure beneath. With his feet positioned either side of the growing trench, Gilly crouched with the bucket between his legs, snapping up ragworms before they could bury themselves back into the mud.

'Would you look at the size of that cunt!' he hooted gleefully, holding a violently wriggling specimen up for inspection. To my eye, there was no change out of nine inches long.

'Jaysus, me aul' fella makes this look easy in the garden,' I huffed after ten minutes, my forearms and shoulders on fire with the effort of digging.

'Here, gimme that shaggin' thing,' said Gilly, grabbing the fork off me. 'Me granny'd dig faster than you. Take the bucket and try to keep up with me.'

Wielding the fork with a feral energy, he began digging like a man possessed, the trench quickly lengthening as I scrambled after him to collect up the exposed ragworms. It went this way for a while, the effort of digging soon dripping from the end of his nose.

'Here, we'll take a break,' I suggested after a good bit. 'We've near four hundred picked.'

'No time,' he replied, mopping his brow with the sleeve of his jumper.

'But I'm banjaxed,' I said, rubbing at the ache along my lower back.

'The tide's comin' back in. We need to make the best of it.'

And with that he set to work digging a fresh trench, powering the fork downwards into the mud as if attempting to spear some giant underground creature.

'Here, go easy with that bloody thing,' I said nervously, whipping my hand back just in time as he came down swiftly with the fork again. 'Give me a chance to pick the damn things up.'

'Ah, stop givin' out, Lar. Just think about the pay day and fill that bucket.'

Taking his advice, I began musing upon the various pleasant ways to blow twenty quid when a tine of the fork skewered the back of my right hand with a soft crunching sound, instantly pinning me to the ground. My knees folded as my free hand dropped the bucket, its writhing contents tipping out into the trench around me. I felt nothing at first, was only vaguely aware of the fork standing vertical as Gilly just gawped at me, both hands to his face.

'AH, LAR! I'M SORRY! JAYSUS, I DIDN'T MEAN IT, I DIDN'T SEE YOUR HAND!' His voice was on the edge of tears, an unfamiliar panicky sound coming from him.

Sure, that couldn't be my hand, I thought looking back down, a mad giggle flying out of me as the image of a kebab flashed through my head – not the doner sort, you understand, but the type you see on a barbecue with the sharp stick poked through the meat. Then the pain kicked in, a white-hot bolt of agony shooting out from the hand that wasn't mine straight up my arm to register in my brain, my vision darkening with the intensity of it. A warm dribble of piss ran down my thigh to meet the cold seawater soaking into the knees of my jeans. Blood quickly welled up around the tine of the fork and began spilling over to pool in the mud and I suddenly felt a fierce desire to puke. A tennis ball covered in dog slobber casually bounced into the trench then, rolling over the newly liberated ragworms, and seconds later I felt the warm panting breath of a dog near my face as if it was pleading with me to throw the ball again. And just before passing out, I heard another panicked voice, a grown-up voice: 'Ah, holy Jaysus, what's after happenin' here, lads? What in God's name have yiz done?'

I woke up in the hospital three days later feeling like a septic tank. My right hand resembled an inflated rubber glove. It throbbed miserably when I tried to wiggle my fingers. My parents were sitting on either side of the bed, Mam clutching a well-used hankie, her poor eyes and nose rubbed raw.

'You're after scaring the living daylights out of us,' she said. 'You're very lucky to be alive. You ended up getting a woeful infection from that fork. They sometimes dump the sewerage nearby where you were digging.'

'Thank God for that dog walker,' my father chimed in. 'If he hadn't gotten the ambulance called as quickly as he did ...' He just shook his head and exhaled.

They peppered me then with talk about antibiotics and sepsis, ligaments and nerve damage. I could look forward to two months of painful physio for my hand, they warned me.

'That Gilligan lad is a bloody scourge,' I overheard my father grumbling when he thought I'd dropped off to sleep again. 'I never liked him. If he ever shows up at our house again I'll kick ten shades of shite out of him.'

'Go easy, Jim,' said Mam, 'his father will deal with him. Besides, there was a pair of them in it.'

'That whole family are a complete shower of wasters. I've a good mind to sue. I don't want our Laurence hanging around with him anymore.'

And that was that. Gilly wasn't let visit me in the hospital and I was warned against ever hanging around with him again, that he was a bad influence. But I ran into him in the school corridor a fortnight later.

'I'm sorry, man,' he said, motioning nervously towards my bandaged hand. 'Does it hurt?'

'What do you think?' I replied, holding my hand up accusingly.

'Fair enough, I s'pose,' he muttered to the floor. 'I didn't mean it, Lar. Swear to God.'

My gaze moved over his face then, taking in the mottled fading evidence of his father's fists, his eyes silently pleading for forgiveness.

'Don't worry about it,' I said. 'Sure, haven't I been excused from doing written homework for the next six weeks because of the physio.'

'Ah, that's fuckin' deadly, man,' said Gilly, brightening up.

'It could be worse,' I replied.

'Maybe I'll catch you around sometime then, yeah?' said Gilly.

The question just hung awkwardly in the air between us until the bell went a few moments later. I gave him some excuse about needing to go down to the infirmary to get my dressing changed, that my hand still hurt like a fecker. He nodded in understanding and sloped off in the opposite direction towards woodwork.

And it still pains me all these years later, damaged nerves that sporadically spark alive to curl my hand into a tight fist. No great fan of the pills, I sometimes use an ointment to treat it, a balm from Holland & Barrett made from a marine mussel extract of all things. I often smile at the irony of this, although my wife can't abide the reek of the stuff. Starting with the palm, I knead the ointment into the old wound, a gossamer-thin patch of smooth skin where my life and fate lines seem to have been sanded away. Then turning my hand over, I rub the ointment into the pale puckered dimple where the fork impaled the back of my hand, smiling inwardly as I trace my thumb along the length of the savage-looking ragworm that now squirms out of my hand through the dimple to wind and slither its way back up along my wrist for evermore. Bad influence or fond remembrance; that's the thing about tattoos – like old scars, they don't wash off.

Campsie Fells, 14th December

Morag Smith

When yer dead, yer dust. There's nuthin' else darlin'
The seasons stop as your birthday rises
like the mountain before us in a brutal
midday that feels like night. We wait
for the mist to decide which way to go.
Your old map softens, tears in our hands.
That path you mentioned sucks our words
into its edges – slick rock and mud,
scrape of boots, rasp and steam of breath
as the slope steepens. Scree
tumbles as we break through low cloud,
then stop, floating on a sea of winter
and cast you to infinite blue.
The gale shoves us down into fog
and moss-slimed frost until the sudden crunch
of car park gravel, thawing of fingers.
Our golden bubble speeds west, the day
spreads its wings and leaves – no ghosts or angels,
just the warm sting of living.

Nature is a Haunted House

Siobhan Campbell

Out on High Street, Amherst, there's an inkling.
An insect-hung breath moves among stones, seeps
into soils, trips along rafters where bats are hiding.
On the space between tree trunks, winter's debris,
the cold that burns has cracked the earth open.
Yet, just above, at tips of branches, is a greening.
Mid-April, not yet Spring in western Massachusetts.
But in that breathing is the intimation, is the wait
and the arrival. The riddle she set is met.

ii

Today, humidity makes a frizz fest of my hair,
I will go to CVS for beeswax smoother.
Walking up High Street, sudden cherry blossom –
when did this happen? And there, buttercups and
geranium about to bloom with reddening flowers.
All this as I pass your house, the Homestead.
E.D. (if I may), I fancy you are at an upper window
looking out past the valley to the Berkshire hills,
not thinking of this Easter day, but seeing the
colouring all the same, a rainbow flag on the First
Congregational Church across the road.

Second Sleep

Enda Coyle-Greene

This is where I begin, in the light of the stars
whose dust falls through air cooled and blued
in the stasis our eyes make of that past-
midnight black, where I find
the atoms that divide inside me ceaselessly
as those aeons-away, dead-already
flickerings our ancestors knew
after sky, lamp, candle
blew themselves out or were snuffed
as the last of the household settled down
on straw or feather bed among the muffled
shufflings of hoof, foot, paw;
and it is here, at a time decided on by no one,
they awoke to love or talk or eat, cold
grates were raked and sparks ignited —
here, now, where a thought is
traced against a word inside a line
I'll try to keep with me beyond this interim
before my second sleep, stalled
like smoke on its journey skywards.

The Last Cuppa

Emily Cullen

On Holy Thursday
the full moon over Holycross Abbey,
a giant Eucharist in the sky.
I try to recall our Last Supper
before you were burdened with your cross
we were forced to keep apart.
We didn't know that cup of coffee
snatched as soon as restrictions lifted
would be our Gethsemane.
On Sunday, I drag my family
to mass for the hope of an empty
tomb, first Easter without you.

The Bind

David Butler

I KNEW THE MINUTE I heard a body'd been found beyond in Graiguecullen, that it was Ruby done it. I knew, sure as if he'd told me he was planning it. Which he pretty much did, one way of looking at it. That's what has me in the bind I'm in.

He come out here about a week. Sure I hadn't seen hide nor hair of the fucker in months. Was a time you wouldn't of seen one of us propping up *The Pikeman* or *Bridge Tavern* without the other was there too. But that was before I took the crack to the skull in the county final we lost to the Crokes. Fractured my eye-socket it did, and the next thing the eye gets infected. After they took the eye I was never any use at judging the flight and dip of the *sliotar*.

So that was that, game over for muggins here. Things went belly-up with Trish about then, too, and the worst I can say on that subject is it was my own stupid fault on account of I spent the next six months sulking and taking it out on her till she'd had enough and broke off the engagement. Course then the following year they went on and won the county final, the feckers. Which was alright, I was happy for them. Genuinely I was. Only Ruby now being captain, it was him as'd be filling the trophy with punch and making the speeches and quips that by rights I'd of been making if it hadn't of been for Stumpy Corrigan's dirty pull that cost me a lot more than the county final so it did.

All that happened a long time ago and it's old history now and I wouldn't be bringing it up only it'll give an idea how surprised I was to hear Ruby Reilly's boy-racer gunning into the yard there last Tuesday week. 'Howya, head?' he goes with a big stupid grin on the bollox as if the seven years in between had never happened and he hadn't married Trish Kelleher. 'Still swinging the devil by the tail?' he goes. But I could tell how shook he was underneath by the palsied fingers dropping the car-keys, and how his eyes flitted about the farm and wouldn't settle on my one eye.

'What has you out this way?' I ask all business-like, no intention of making things easy for the fucker. 'Can't a man drop out anymore for a social call or what the hell way is the country gone?' and we might of gone on talking shite all evening only his phone plinked and I seen him flinch when he clocked who the message was from. Then at last he looks square at me and goes 'Look-it, Patch, we need to talk, can we go somewhere?' I was back living at home this long time, and he didn't want the oul dear earwigging on whatever it was he had to tell me. 'Will we go for a sneaky one?' says I, for I've a quare thirst on me these days. 'I'd as soon go for a walk,' says he, and I knew then it was a serious business had brung him out. I wish to God now I told him where he could go with his serious business but there we are, with hindsight as the fella says.

Long story short, he'd got himself in with this quare wan beyond in Graigue. Things hadn't been going so well with Trish, not since his oul fella's business went tits-up last March. They were God knows how many months behind on the mortgage repayments. Has a bit of a temper on him, Ruby, and the dogs on the street knew Trish was living back with her people out in Leighlinbridge. Now I should say, by the time Ruby Reilly and Trish Kelleher got hitched a couple of years back, I was over her. If I didn't go to the wedding itself, it wasn't because I wasn't invited. It was that I'd gone off the rails drinking at the time and I'd of probably made a show of myself once the demon drink got a hold. Because one thing I'll say, whether it's on account of the PTSD or whatever they do call it, after losing the eye the drink does send me into a dark place an odd time. Which is why I'm barred out of *The Pikeman*. Which is saying something.

So Ruby tells me this quare wan from beyond in the Graigue is ringing and texting him ever since, and won't leave him alone. 'Ever since what?' says I and the squint he throws me is as much as to say wouldya cop onto yourself you know well what. So then I ask him what was he thinking, getting involved with some brasser in the first place because one thing I'll say for Trish Kelleher, she's never lost it. If I wasn't jealous of the bollox marrying her, it's only because I've always wanted the pure best for Trish. I couldn't of stood the idea she might of gone through with marrying me on account of she felt sorry for me losing the eye.

Like I say, I can be my own worst enemy.

'Look-it, Patch. My head was all over the shop. Trish and myself was after having this big bust-up. Not just on account of the mortgage either, that's all I can say on the subject. Then she gets on her high horse and moves back in with her folks up in Leighlinbridge. So I'm out one night in *The Dungeon* acting the eejit with a few of the lads and I've a feed of drink on me, and I'm outside having a smoke when this oul wan starts giving me the sympathetic ear and I dunno what devil got into me Patch I mean she's no spring chicken, anything but, but the next thing I'm back in her gaff so I am and I'm that angry with Trish at the time that I think fuck it. *Fuck* it. And now I can't get shot of her, she's ringing and texting all hours. Then yesterday, right? She threatens she'll call out to Leighlinbridge to introduce herself to Trish if I don't meet up with her! I swear to you, I'm that close to ...' His next words, whatever they were, were strangled by the rage.

'Well?' says I. 'Where do I come into any of this?' Though I knew well enough the way Ruby's mind was calculating. Couple of months after the business with the eye-socket, Ruby Reilly and a bruiser by the name of Dinny Foley set on Stumpy Corrigan one night with a couple of hurls, though he's a brick shithouse of a fucker. Long and short of it was he never played senior hurling again. And I was delighted, coz he was one dangerous fucker, had a reputation for throwing the *sliotar* right up into your face before pulling across it. Dinny Foley's out in Australia this long time. All the same I knew well, before ever he said it, that Ruby had that whole business with Stumpy Corrigan in mind when he come out to see me. 'All I want you to do is put the frighteners on her. Just give her one dacent fright is all. Pull on a balaclava. Smash a couple of flowerpots. Put in the windshield of her car. Only be sure she sees you doing it.' 'Why don't you do it yourself?' 'She'd have the guards on me is why. She works for Rhatigan? The lawyer? So I'll have to have a watertight alibi for the night you're doing it.' 'I'm not doing it.' 'You're not?' 'I'm not scaring some biddy out of her wits for you, Ruby.' 'It wouldn't be for me. It'd be for Trish.' 'For Trish. How d'you figure that?' 'Think about it!' That was Ruby all over. Twisting an argument backways so it was never Ruby Reilly was at fault. And that's what did it for me. After that there was no way on God's Earth I was doing a turn for him, with his 'It'd be for Trish'.

So when I heard a woman's body'd been found up beyond in Graiguecullen, I knew well it was Ruby done it. Then yesterday he calls out again! You believe the cunt? I hear his boy-racer growling along for a country mile before he pulls into the yard. 'Get in,' he goes, not deigning to look at me. I do, I couldn't tell you why, and off he speeds, skidding round the backroads of Carlow like a demented rally-driver, and he that agitated he won't look at me while he explains what happened. Course none of it's his fault. His head is literally all over the shop by the time he's out in her place, threating her if she goes next or near Leighlinbridge what he won't do to her and her precious cocker-spaniel Pixie.

And then she tells him she's pregnant.

'Christ's sake she's pushing fifty! There's no way she's *pregnant*. And after, what? Three *weeks*, like? But she swears blind, and this lecherous leer on her puss, I swear to you Patch, if you seen it! So I seen red. She has me that agitated that instead of taking a swipe at her telly like I intended, I let fly at her with the hurl and I must of caught her on the temple or something because she went down and she never got up again.'

Suddenly he's pulling a handbrake and spitting up gravel out by the quarry and the force has me thrown flat again the door before we stop. He sits stock-still, white-knuckles gripping the wheel, his eyes big as gobstoppers. What he says next is deathly calm. 'If you done what I asked you, none of this hada happened.'

'Why are you telling me this?'

He looks at me like I'm a right spastic. He pokes a finger into my chest – there's no shake today – and he goes, 'I was with you all last night, is why.' 'Where?' 'I don't give a fuck where, Patch. Wherever you want.' 'I was home with the old dear all last night.' 'Then I was with yiz. *You* tell her, yeah?' 'I'm not bringing the mother into this. No way.' 'Ok. So then we were somewhere's else. I don't give a ...' 'Why me? Couldn't you not ask someone else, Ruby?' 'You, I'm asking.' 'But why?' 'Because you're the only one knows. And that makes you an accessory, *a chara*. You're an accessory before *and* after the fact.' 'How d'you figure that?' 'Because I told you all about her, Patch. I told you before I done it. And I'm telling you again, now. Eyes of the law, that makes you an accessory.'

So there it is. The bind I'm in. Fucked if I know what I'm supposed to do.

I could just go to the guards, tell them what I know. I mean, he never actually *said* he was going to lay a finger on her. As for him telling me afterwards, how does that make me guilty? For listening, like?

But if word got out I'm turned grass, Jesus! Coz I'd be called on to give evidence. Then say he wasn't convicted, strength of my word alone, see what I'm saying?

Simplest would be, go along with what he's asking. The ole dear's not going to know, I can leave her well out of it. But then, like I say, I've always acted in Trish Kelleher's best interests. That's why I didn't stand in the way when first she hooked up with Ruby Reilly. But do I really want her to go back to him, and he a murderer? And worse again, one that done the dirt on her.

You Can't Go Back

Barbara De Franceschi

to right the wrongs of childhood,
the weft is stretched,
hurts perceived weaken the weave.
The memoir keeps writing itself,
blame drifts on a paper boat,
instinct and exaggeration
go up and down on waves of misty recall.
Reality is a rabbit pulled from a hat:
illusion mixed with trickery.
To untangle the shadows
you have to stop skipping,
get off the merry-go-round,
put your marbles away,
and live with the silence.

Coffee Morning, Herbert Park

Maurice Devitt

Though it's a cold November day
the low sun entices them outside,
to sit in a scrum around a picnic table,
the lone smoker adrift at the end
of the bench. There is a strict sequence
to their conversation, opening with
an update on their ailments, progressing
to the rugby at the weekend, a roll call
of grandchildren and an update
on former colleagues. As work stories
unfold, the table is divided.
Some, effusive up till then, lapse
into silence, perhaps remembering
what they did, or what was done to them.

Constellations

Clive Donovan

The world turns somehow
but when the clouds clear,
night's sky is different:
Gone are the bears,
major and minor,
the scorpion, crab and all that crowd
of bull, ram, goat, no more;
the water carrier, dubious scales
and the alleged twins.
Even doughty Orion,
with easy-to-spot sword belt
and snapping dog at heel,
is gone. A new configuration
of constellations
is apparent up there: I see
a weeping unicorn in flight
and a dove feeds upon spare stars
and two hands clasp in a handshake
in the dark; a whip, a stick;
a fractured heart:
Everything and nothing is changed.

Through The Window A Magpie

Lisa Frank

THROUGH THE CRACK in the curtain a triangle of light shines on the baby blue sheet nestled between their bodies. Claire traces its lines from one edge to another, its point like an arrow shooting up towards Tom's face. As she stares at the crown of his lips, noticing for the first time the way one side seems more rounded than the other, she thinks about what people would say if they knew. *It's wrong.* Of course they'd say that. *And how could they? Don't they realise what they've done?*

Wrong. She'd never felt so close to that word before, its legs pinning her into a corner she can't scoot out of. It isn't until she hears a magpie cawing in the garden that Claire finally turns away. She closes her eyes, imagining it creeping its way through the white rhododendrons, pecking at the leaves as it makes its way through to the wet grass. It caws again, louder this time, and she wonders _ as she always does – why it is that they always sound so aggrieved. Like the whole world is out to get them. She opens her eyes and looks back at Tom.

She tries to remember how it started, the one thing that led to the next. Maybe when his hand brushed her hair away from her face, the slight flutter of his finger against her skin. Or when he patted away the tears from her cheek, the familiar trace of lavender soap whirling around in the space between them. Or was it when she put her hand on his, holding it there, perhaps a few seconds too long. It's then she questions whether there was some deep-down part of her that wanted it to happen. That willed it. It had been so long, the feeling of skin on skin reminding her that there was still — after all these years — a living want inside of her. And so without any thought of right or wrong, her body gave into it, settling into his, the loneliness that had been festering inside her for all those years now finally subsided. Thinking about it as she watches Tom sleep, Claire wonders how something that felt so natural, like it was meant to happen, could be so wrong.

*

Jack waits until Áine is settled in the bath before he reaches into the back of his underwear drawer for his cigarettes. He fishes one out, sticks it behind his ear and puts the pack back in its hiding place.

'I'm taking out the bins,' he says as he passes the bathroom door and then shuffles down the stairs and out the front. After dragging the bins to the kerb, he finally lights the cigarette. But just as he takes his first drag, he looks up and sees the opened bathroom window. *To hell with it*, he thinks. *Let her smell damn smoke; I'm a grown man, after all.* But a moment later he crosses the road, deciding it isn't worth the headache. If only the kids hadn't moved out he could blame it on them, like he used to, and wouldn't have to cross the road to stand in front of the neighbour's house.

He's halfway through the cigarette when he hears something like a cry coming from inside the neighbour's house. He takes a peek through the window and sees some sort of movement but without his glasses it's too hard to see. The sound gets louder and so he takes a quick look around and then tiptoes closer to the house to get a better look. He sees Mrs Cronin lying naked on the floor, a man moving on top of her, her arms wrapped around his back. Jack watches for a moment, then scurries back across the road, taking note of the new red hatchback parked behind Mrs Cronin's house.

After sticking the cigarette butt into the bin, he sneaks back into the house, wondering if he should tell Áine that Mrs Cronin finally got herself a boyfriend, one with a fondness for red hatchbacks. But in the end he goes to bed, deciding to keep his secrets to himself. *Good for old Mrs Cronin*, he thinks as he starts drifting off to sleep. *And on the living room floor, no less.*

In the morning, after giving Áine a quick peck on the cheek, Jack grabs his rusted green travel mug and goes to the car, every morning the same. Just as he fastens his seatbelt, his mobile phone beeps with his morning messages. He's scrolling through them when he sees a man leaving through the side door of Mrs Cronin's house. Jack hunkers down, waiting to get a look at the man. The red car is quick to drive away but Jack recognised the man's face.

He throws down his phone and races back into the house, where Áine is scrubbing down the kitchen counter.

'Do you know if Tom Keenan got a new car?' Jack says.

Áine turns around, hand steady on her heart.

'What? What are you doing back—'

'Tom Keenan, did he get a new car, do you know?'

She motions to Claire Cronin's house across the road.

'You mean *that* Tom Keenan?'

'Yes, of course *that* Tom Keenan,' Jack says, hearing his voice as if it's someone else's. 'Did he get a new car or not?'

Áine puts down her sponge.

'Yes, a little red Toyota, I think.'

Jack takes a seat at the table.

'Have I a story for you.'

Áine has only barely sat down and Jack already has the whole story out, not even bothering to care about what she'd say about his sneaky cigarette. Áine looks at him, then out the window towards Mrs Cronin's house, then back at him again.

'With her own brother, are you sure?'

'I'm sure.'

She looks out the window again, seeing a magpie feasting on the cherry tree.

'Whatever you do,' she says, ' just don't spread it around.'

*

Sean and his friend Charlie are huddled behind the old brick university canteen, a joint passing between them. Catriona is there too, wearing her tall black boots that Sean can't get enough of. He's trying not to stare, all the while doing his best to think of something witty to say. But as usual, he's coming up dry. He kicks at the acorns that line the ground, hoping he doesn't look as awkward as he feels.

'You'll never guess what my da just told me,' he says.

Charlie takes a drag off the joint.

'What's that?'

'You remember Mrs Cronin from school?'

'The Pythagorean theorem,' Charlie says with a roll of his eyes. 'She was always on about that.'

'That's right,' Sean laughs.

'She's been taking Mammy's aqua aerobics class for years, ever since her husband died,' Catriona says and looks over at Sean. 'What about her?'

'She lives across the road from my parents,' he says with a pause, wondering if he should mention how Mrs Cronin bakes them a lemon drizzle cake every Christmas or how she used to slip him a tenner for mowing her lawn, even though his da said he was to do it for free. But he decides to go straight to the story. 'She's getting it on with her brother.'

'Oh, my ...' Catriona says, handing the joint to Sean.

'Tom Keenan?' Charlie laughs. 'He does our taxes.'

'Mammy always says how nice Mrs Cronin is,' Catriona says. 'They have the chats in the changing room after the pool.'

'What are they even having sex for at their age anyway?' Charlie says.

Sean laughs and passes the joint to Catriona. 'They're not *that* old.'

'They turned seventy-five last year,' Catriona says. 'Mammy tried to get Mrs Cronin to have a party.'

'*They*?' Charlie says. 'What do you mean, like, twins?'

'Yeah, twins,' Catriona says.

'That's even worse,' Charlie says. 'It's like fucking yourself.'

They all laugh.

Sean starts kicking at the acorns again. From the corner of his eye he can see Catriona watching him. He kicks one over to her. She stops it with her foot.

*

Through the reflection in the mirror Maria glances at the cat, a fifteen-year-old ginger fellow that loves nothing better than to roll around in the sun. She has to keep an eye out for him, scared that the magpies will come after him again. She turns back to Catriona.

'Just taking off the ratty bits?'

Catriona touches the bottom of her hair for split ends.

'I think maybe a good inch this time.'

'Good girl,' Maria says and asks how Catriona's courses are going as she combs out her hair. Catriona tells her about all the reading and how she wishes she didn't have to live at home. Just as Catriona starts telling her about a boy, Maria hears the magpies.

'Just a sec,' Maria says and runs out to the garden, the smell of fresh-cut grass catching in her nose. The magpies shriek and then fly off. Maria goes over to the cat and gives him a quick rub before going back inside.

'Sorry about that,' she says and starts combing out Catriona's hair again. 'So, any craic?'

'I did just hear the weirdest story,' she says. 'You know Mrs Cronin, the old maths teacher at the secondary school?'

'A bob,' Maria says. 'Always an A-line bob to her chin. Course I haven't seen her in a while now. Don't tell me she has cancer.'

'No,' Catriona says, catching Maria's eye in the mirror. 'That's not it.'

*

Claire lifts her hand away from the keyboard, the arthritis stiffening her fingers. But she's not in the mood to answer emails anyway. Her mind keeps drifting. She finds herself thinking about moving away. Australia, she thinks, or maybe Greece. No one cares what you do in Greece. From the money they'd get from selling their houses and what she has saved, they could go anywhere.

No one will ever know, she'll tell Tom. *We'll move away and live as we like. We can be happy then.*

*

Maria finds herself thinking about Claire Cronin as she cracks an egg into a pan, remembering how nice she had been to her nephew, Simon, who is dyslexic and used to jumble up the numbers. 'She has the patience of a saint,' her sister used to say. And so what if she's shagging her brother. They're not hurting anyone, especially not at their age. And besides, who am I to judge? Maria decides that she'll keep this one to herself. But then the magpies start in again and she feels her nerves take hold of her and the next thing she knows she's telling her 4:30 cut-and-colour.

'The things that happen in this town,' Maria says.

*

Tom has sat in his car the better part of an hour thinking of what he'll say to her. How to begin. Eventually he drags himself out and makes his way to her house, each step so firm and final in its place.

'Good evening, Mr Keenan,' a voice calls from across the road. Tom turns to see Claire's neighbour Jack sitting on a bench doing a crossword, pretending it's a usual thing for him to do. It's then Tom knows. *He knows.*

*

Claire sits across the table from Tom, listening as he tells her that it can never happen again.

'Sure, it's wrong,' he says and starts picking at his cuticles, just as he did when he was little.

Claire turns and looks out the window, seeing the flickering light of the TV screen in the house across the road, every single night the same. She stares at it, deciding that after Tom leaves, she'll gather all her pills, pour herself a double brandy and fill the bath tub up high.

'Okay,' she says, turning to Tom, knowing he'll be out the door in seconds flat.

Swearing Stone

Billy Fenton

In the time before we could write
words on paper, before rings, before
melting wax, I stood before a stone.
Light cut through the drizzle
in his hair like the dew on a spider's
web trapping an early sun.
He pushed his arm through the centre
of the stone, through the carved cross
as if he was calling out for love.
I took his hand – damp as a slug –
it tightened around mine. I heard him
say yes. I heard my voice say yes.
He took me to his hut. Outside,

feasting, music, as he pounded
on top of me – two tribes now one.
The eye of this stone has seen promises
that were kept. Raged its curse
on promises that were broken.
But what of the promises that were
never in the heart – forced –
to forge a history. Does it know?
As a robin knows to eat a worm,
or a river knows to flow to the sea,
or a baby knows when to be born.
I look back as I re-take the Western Road,
the glow of morning in its waiting eye.
The gallop of hooves in the distance.

A swearing stone or 'leac na mionn' in Irish ('stone of the oaths'), is a holed standing stone used in early Ireland. Accounts of how they were used vary. Some are still extant.

The Day the Satellites Went Down

Cian Ferriter

His car engine was still running,
miles from where they found him.
A trail of sorts in his wake –
muddied shoe, phone glinting
like a dropped earring, jacket suspended
from a branch like a small life.
No-one could work out why
he chose that spot. Never more alive,
he said, later. Crown of his head
pressed through the gap, fern-fronds
like jump-leads against his temples,
his tongue lapping the black juice of the bog.
Still talked about in the office.
From the desk that used to be his,
I replay the scene: low gasps, light breeze,
the soft pink soles of his feet
quivering like a new-born
filling his lungs with alien air.

Pleasure

Joel Fishbane

QUARANTINE'S BEEN HELL and for weeks we've replaced Netflix-and-Chill with Avoidance-and-Terse-Remarks. I've gotten used to grumping around. Then Wash surprises me. There's a dance show at an amphitheatre. People sit in roped-off areas. The show lasts thirty minutes and is once an hour until late. Not quite wine and romance but I haven't gone further than the pharmacy since the spring. And at least he's making an effort. I decide to show some faith.

Then I see the show.

'Those dancers were sensational,' says Wash.

'Sure.'

As we leave, Wash walks a little too close. Wash is overprotective and it's only gotten worsen since the virus. As if he can throw himself between it and me. I used to like that about him. A walking shield to protect me from the world.

'You lack an appreciation for art.'

'I liked it.'

'It hardly sounds like it.'

'The patios are full. Let's eat in the park.'

We get banh mi and find a spot in the grass. I use my sweater as a blanket and we huddle as we eat. Our masks dangle like pirate earrings. His breath is mayonnaise and lime.

'Your problem,' he says, 'is anhedonia. It means you can't feel pleasure.'

'I know what it means.'

'You are suffering from social withdrawal.'

'I like the sandwiches.'

'But not the dancers.'

'When you go to the dentist, are you amazed when she cleans your teeth? The dancers aren't worth conversation. They gave me exactly what I expected.'

'I took you out. I thought you'd be happy.'

'You took me to a show starring your little Zoom friend. It's a small apartment, Wash. You think I don't know what's going on?'

His brow frowns. His receding hairline is an attacking one and it's coming for his eyes and nose and me. He retreats behind his mask. Now he's a bandit, the sort who robs travellers of gold and lovers of months of their life.

'It's just internet love.'

'That's what you said last time. You're a dentist, you know that?'

'What the hell does that mean?'

'All you do is clean my teeth.'

'You're the one that sticks around. What does that say about you? Don't pretend you're going anywhere. Unhappiness is a virus too.'

He's right, of course. I could have confronted him as soon as I found out. I could have gone to my sister's. A packed suitcase has been in the closet since March. But I just stayed inside like one of the condemned.

At home, Wash laughs when I pull the suitcase free. 'I'm going to bed. I'll see you in the morning.'

I want him to be wrong. The world and its dangers aren't going anywhere. We might as well learn to get along. At the window, I put my bare face against the glass. I'm not smiling yet but it's there on the corners. Anxious as I am. Trying to get free.

Mycelium

Bernadette Gallagher

A mushroom, its head above the ground,
threads below casting a web –
carrying water to the roots of oak, ash, hazel.

We gorge on *truffle*, admire *chanterelle*
and avoid the enticing *fly agaric*.

Thread from baby to mother, that cord, though
broken, still connected by an unseen strand of tissue.
A forest floor erupts, love is always here.

Natives

Kevin Graham

Your hand's in mine as in a song,
its tune the catch of what's gone wrong
but also what is right in the world:
this tenement of longing
for living in the actual moment,
like one sparkler lighting off another.
How rich to hunker by a fallen trunk
and have fern-fronds tickle your wrist
over a blanket of moist, dead leaves.
Look how dark green ivy twists
in a flutter of life
and the ladybird clings stock still
waiting for our shadows to lift
like clouds above an idyll.

The Writing of a Letter in a Hostel in a Mountain Pass at Night

Richard W. Halperin

The moon is a companion.
My pen glides across the page.
The letter may never be read,
may never be delivered.
For now, happiness.
A good letter. Not about me,
not about him. Not about the weather.
'Is it to Derry?' someone asks.
'I don't know a Derry,' I say.
I don't mind the interruption.
I do not know where I am going
tomorrow, but I have this night.
I am not dead yet. My brain
is not-bad tonight. My brain
is not-bad.

Career Path

Joanne Hayden

AGE 5, PALAEONTOLOGIST

Yesterday in the park Sam dawdled to dig through leaves with a stick. Trillions of leaves, orange and crunchy, mushier underneath. Snug in his gloves and dino jacket. His breath made smoke in the air, shooting shapes that tumbled and curled and disappeared before *one, two, thr*.... He dug up an empty crisp packet and a ketchup-slobbered box. Could barely hear the others, was like being alone in the world. Scary and fun, the same tummywobbles as before he jumped off the too-high wall.

Ellie came back. He knew she would. First he saw her legs and feet. She bent down. Her cheeks were red. Seethrough snot dribbled onto her lips. She magicked a tissue from under her sleeve.

'Maybe you'll find an antler,' she said. Once they'd found a pigeon fossil in their garden and another time a broken plate. Ellie told their mum the plate was Palaeolithic and to ring the woman who did the news.

Yesterday Ellie dug with her hands and splashed him on purpose with leaves. 'Oakfetti,' she said.

'Bury me.' Sam lay down. 'I want oakfetti up to my head.'

Ellie didn't bury him. She lay on the leafy bed too and they twisted their heads so they were staring at each other.

'Let's make leaf angels,' she said.

He copied how she moved her arms and legs, clearing the leaves into wings, him and Ellie laughing and flying till their dad came huffing back, saying, 'C'mon will you, Mum's gone ahead, we're going to look at the president's house.'

They looked at the president's gates and the president's fence and the president's thorny moat. Then they went to the tearooms. Warm, but Sam kept his jacket on so the stegs and T-rexes and pterosaurs could see what was happening: his mum queuing at the counter, his dad opening a paper someone had left behind.

Sam used his phonics to try and read a word. 'What's *uh-turn*?' he said.

'*You* turn,' his dad said.

'The opposite of *me* turn,' Ellie said.

His dad laughed. 'My me turn is your you turn.'

They were teasing Sam and leaving him out and that wasn't kind or fair because Ellie was three years older than him and could understand reading jokes but he didn't whinge or tell them to stop, he climbed up onto his dad's knee and taught them a tongue twister he'd learned in school: sheep should sleep in a shed.

His mum brought the hot chocolates. Ellie plonked her marshmallows into Sam's cup.

'Since when do you not like marshmallows?' his mum said.

'Since a quarter past nine this morning,' Ellie said, and Sam's mum told him he had a marshmallow moustache and he told her he was giving the day a thousand out of ten.

Age 10, Wizard

He'd finished with these books a year ago so why was he flicking through them again? Lying in bed instead of at his desk but Mum never checked his homework anymore. Too busy with work and worryanger, always in Ellie's room going on about love and, 'Talk to me, El, it's so important to talk.'

He could hear Mum's footsteps going down the stairs and Ellie turning pages on the other side of the wall, sulking cause now, for her own good, gymnastics was on the Not Allowed list. No running, no press-ups, no star jumps and Dad said they might have to get rid of the trampoline. Sam still used the trampoline. If anyone would notice he'd sulk as well.

Ellie had helped him read these books. The two of them would charge around in their cloaks, pointing their wands and shouting. They used to know all the spells. Ones for water and light. Forgetting. Was there a spell to make someone want to eat?

Last night Sam was on his way to the kitchen to get a drink of apple juice. He heard Mum and Dad whisper-arguing and stayed listening at the door.

'So bloody stubborn,' Dad said. 'Always was. Remember as a toddler she wouldn't go to bed? She'd lie rigid on the floor so we couldn't pick her up.'

'It's more complicated than stubbornness,' Mum said. 'We need to be constructive here.'

'How complicated is it,' Dad said, 'to chew and swallow your food? Eat when you're hungry, it's as basic as that. We've given them too much choice.'

'We meaning *me*?'

'Seriously? You're going to make this about yourself?'

A year ago Sam's bedroom walls were covered with posters from the films, wizards duelling, the flying car, Undesirable Number One. Now there was just the Liverpool team and a sign saying This is Anfield and the marks the Blu-tack had left behind. He was embarrassed he'd been so obsessed.

He dropped the books. Seven thumps. An idea landed in his head.

Mum had kept the toy cooker. 'For my grandchildren,' she'd said. It was in the spare room on top of the filing cabinets. He made steps from two of the drawers, tricky to climb but he made it. The plastic food was still there – in the oven on a tray. He threw it all down and went to knock on Ellie's door.

'Go away,' she said in a sniffly voice.

'It's me,' he said.

'Fine.'

He walked to her desk, holding the tray, feeling like he needed to pee. She stared and stared at the fake food, her eyes bubbling in her bony face. She might shout. Worse, maybe she'd cry but she smiled and turned back to herself and the prickles left his chest and disappeared from the room as though someone had let in air.

She picked up the cheese, 'Yum,' put it in her mouth.

There was no spell to make it real. He knew the magical laws. Food couldn't be conjured up from nothing and even if it could he wouldn't prank her like that.

She spat the holey triangle across the room. Nearly hit the radiator.

'Some haddock, sir?' She pointed to the tray. He put the whole fish into his mouth, chewed as long as he could then shot it almost as far as the cheese. A cookie for her, a lemon for him. They turned their mouths into pellet guns. Chewing and spitting until Ellie's carpet looked like after the food fight in school and they were interrupted by Mum coming in with slices of real cheese and bread.

Age 15, Mountaineer

The iron steps clanged under Sam's feet. He took them two at a time, harder, faster so that the rings and echoes looped in the purple dark. Up and up, pains in his legs and taste of iron in his throat, his body absorbing the metal of the hospital's fire escape.

Clear out thoughts. Every single. Listen to the thumping in his ears, the beat a kind of music. Pump it. Three at a time. Up and up. Inside they were sitting on opposite sides of her bed, the pair who'd made her, pushed apart; her shadow had grown as she shrank. They must regret it, having kids. Understandable. But he couldn't be in there with their separateness and the animal fur on her arms. The smell of her leaving. Fester beneath the chemicals.

Up and a break. Air getting thin. He needed an oxygen tank. That project he did in primary school about the Sherpa guides. *The Sherpa are an ethnic Tibetan group. Many of them live in Nepal. Mount Everest is between Tibet and Nepal. It is the highest mountain on Earth.* The view from here, halfway up, car lights white and red, the Dublin mountains in the distance. *Sherpas help climbers reach Everest's peak. They have adapted to high altitudes. They carry luggage and navigate.* Roofs and spires and streetlamps, silhouettes of trees. Colder though. *Sherpas can tell if there's dangerous weather on the way.*

Up again. Different now. Tiredness slowing his pace. Blazing pain. Heart pounding. Still he pushed almost to the top. *It's a bad idea to climb Everest without a Sherpa guide.* Enough. He sat. His Sherpa was deserting, had pretty much already gone and he didn't want a replacement. Last month he'd texted Dee. *Can't handle us right now need 2 take a break.* Nothing for a day then she'd got back. *OK Sam I understand.* He wished she'd been angry, left shouty voicemails, bitched about him to their friends. Yesterday another flash on the screen. She must've heard what was happening. *Here if u want 2 talk as friends. Call me anytime.*

He took out his phone and deleted Dee's message, looked between the steps. A long way down, a short drop to end this bursting of his head. What Ellie had been doing only quicker. No one here to say stop. Over the handrail, let everything go. They'd be minus two kids then and along with the why and why and why rage, he couldn't copy her, that he had to stay, be his own Sherpa, Hillary and Norgay mashed up.

Age 20, Nightwatchman

Almost perfect, his latest gig: protecting a building supplies warehouse in Lichtenberg from timber and copper thieves. A month in and he knew every aisle of plasterboard, every overstacked shelf of paint. Giant rolls of insulation. Bags of concrete mix. Good money and hours that suited, he went to bed when his flatmates got up, left soon after they came back from work. Guaranteed weekend shifts.

He could read on the job, could ignore or respond to the tick tick of messages from home: his mum had talked to admissions, still time to register for his final year, finish his degree blah blah blah, *Let me know when it suits to talk.* Her nagging better than the fake buddiness of his father about to become a father again.

He could play with mastic guns, adjustable wrenches. Perfect but for Radek. Every second night he was paired with Radek who insisted on conversation, on and on about his seven grandkids, sentimentalising his youth in Prague. Radek who said, 'It must be difficult when your father takes a new wife?' Who said, 'You are an only child? You were lonely growing up?'

Radek who was, right now, clearing the monitoring desk and setting it with mugs and plates, forks, a silver flask, napkins printed with different coloured balloons. Slices of cake from a box.

'Medovik,' Radek said.

'You're alright,' Sam said. 'I'm OK.'

'I am alright and you are OK,' Radek said. 'Maybe, maybe not. Either way try my wife's medovik. It was my birthday yesterday.'

Sam had spent his own birthday alone in the *Museum für Naturkunde*, phone switched off, party emojis deferred in favour of fossilised creatures and plants.

'Happy birthday,' he said though the words felt wrong. He sat on a swivel chair. Radek poured coffee from the flask and passed him a slice of cake. Sam stared at the plate, the triangle in the middle, high and dusted with crumbs. He always ate well, no fuss, no skimping, he made a point of it but this cake with its endless, skinny layers and filling in between, almost perfectly symmetrical, was making it difficult to pick up the fork.

'Please,' Radek said.

And it jolted Sam when it hit his tongue, a deep sweetness almost like pain, soft and tangy, whisking him backwards, tasting of when he was a boy, toast and porridge, the special tea, him and Ellie with spoons in the jar, pulling out sticky blobs and trails until the morning she pushed the jar away, skidding it across the table to him without taking off the lid.

He took another bite, put down the fork. Rubbed the back of his neck.

'It is all the honey,' Radek said. 'So much honey. Sometimes it makes me sad too.'

Sam ate slowly, watching the cake change shape with every cut. When it was gone he spoke to the empty plate. 'I wasn't always an only child,' he said.

Grandmother Spider

Ann Howells

Still centre of a turning world, she understands
the unspoken, silences between heartbeats.
Her Buddha smile welcomes those who watch
or weep at night
accepts contradictions & secrets
understands confidence comes easier in darkness
accompanied by a cup of tea.
She spins her silk to ensnare nieces & nephews
grandchildren & great-grandchildren
second cousins once & twice removed.
Grandmother courses their veins:
her double helix a saga,
her body an ear as she turns in white satin silence
to one who barely tolerates her own skin
one whose tears are 80-proof
one hollow & empty as a tin pail.
Grandmother, well into her ninth decade
approaches transcendence. She doesn't like everyone
wouldn't choose half of them, but – good or bad –
they are kin.
She gathers them, heart-sore & mind-weary
over wrought & over medicated –
polygraph slicing to the bone of truth.

Trust, like virtue, can be lost but once.
She whispers secrets to the stars, serenity palpable.
Her incantations heal, sing stones to life,
hang like smoke in wool, never written down.

Calvary

Stephen Shields

Golgotha is to the East;
the pink tinged sky
tries to dispel the night.
We carry swathes of linen.
Our apothecary has furnished
all the spices for embalming:
A powder of myrrh,
Frankincense, canopic
Jars perfumed with herbs.
Prepared for a simple
burial, we are surprised
by the stone rolled back,
an angel armed with light.

The Nearly New Shop

Laura Treacy Bentley

is filled with stories
about last times.
The last time
a faded winter coat
felt a heartbeat.
The last time
a pair of tiny shoes
skipped to school.
The last time
a prom dress
dreamed of love.
The very last time
a chipped coffee cup
caressed human lips.

The Dry Dianthus

Jean Tuomey

My mother leaves home
in an ambulance. We watch
its yellow door slam, blue
lights flash, and she's gone.

The doctor on call suggests
we water the plants on the doorstep.
Her trick of distraction, a reminder –
we must tend what we love.

I recall a visit to the empty house
of a deceased aunt. My father leant over
on his stick, tapped a plant potted
at her locked door, filled a jug with water.

Further unnerved by the lunchtime news –
war in Ukraine could continue for years,
I tighten the grip on my pen, allow words leak –
we must tend what we love.

Parsnip Soup

Ana Reisens

It is my intent to live gently, by which I mean
parsnips cannot grow where there are stones.
Our fingerprints are made of every vegetable
we've ever held, every red velvet bulb and
leafy sprout. We do not always realise this.
Too much is lost in the chewing. The leeks
know where sunshine meets gold,
but who among us had tasted it?
Meanwhile I sip moonbeams from a teaspoon,
soak parsnips in a little bowl. Someday
my bowl will be big enough to hold the sun.
Someday I will make consommé from the rain
and bread from petals, but for now I settle
for whatever I can hold in my hands.

Archive of an Artist

Maria Isakova Bennett

for Michael Wright, Liverpool and Clonakilty

i
A scribble of waves
smoke fumes the angles of cranes
and in the wake of the vessel
lines like grasses growing skywards
up through the river

ii
A crush of clouds and in the distance hills –
maybe Wales
hatching   mid-tone
left-handedness

iii
A man   his body a bag of fabrics
faces Birkenhead
In sight of the Cunard Building –
wings are caught as dots and quick short lines
Aboard a ferry
a smudge   and another
Gradually sun lays itself out
across the river

A ventilation shaft

looms in front of a boat

The man leans forward
    a dark cuboid

   iv
A woman framed
by a fan of charcoal lines
gives herself up
to the elements

    A breeze from the left
causes her hair
partly to obscure her face

     She squints
her hands by her sides

as though told not to interfere
     with what happens next

   v
The page is divided –
seagulls in a chaos of sea-breezes
some in small settlements
on the Coastguard tower
filling the morning   sounding alarms

Along the edge
a child crawls
hair like a dandelion
one hand open   fingers splayed
the other raised
a request or resist

In between all of this –
a couple   their backs to us
hold each other close
wrapped up against
and ready to face
the sea's whip

Kiki

Monica Igoe

I WATCH DIRK BUTTON HIS SHIRT. He's in good shape. Still tanned from Thailand. He pauses. Glances down at me. I pretend to be asleep. It's what he wants.

The door clicks shut and he slips past on the far side of the drenched windowpanes. He cuts a striking figure, the collar of his trench coat upturned, head high.

The conference on *Women in Modern English Literature* doesn't start until 1 pm. I know because I googled it, right after he'd called to say he'd be in Dublin for the weekend. He said it in that syrupy voice that used to make me weak, that he'd missed his Irish woman. I was flattered. I cancelled my shift at the hair salon and drew up a list of things to do together.

I drag myself out of bed, trudge into the damp communal bathroom, and brace myself for the onslaught of cold. The landlord still hasn't fixed the thermostat. Afterwards, I swallow two Solpadeine and dive back beneath the duvet and try to warm up.

And I think about last night.

I'd taken Dirk to a new fish restaurant in Temple Bar. I'd wanted to check it out before, but I'd no-one to go with. We ate loads of seafood back in Thailand, so I considered it an appropriate choice. The restaurant was intimate, ten tables or so, a bit cramped really, the lobster tank so close to our table that every time I looked up, I was confronted with floating crustaceans, their limbs bound with elastic bands. Twice during the night, a waiter fished one out with silver tongs and carried it off on a stainless-steel platter in through the silver double doors into the kitchen. It made me a little sad.

Dirk prized the shell off a crab with the back of his knife, swallowed some pink flesh and pronounced it perfect. 'Try some,' he said. 'Not as salty as in Thailand. Course, the proper way to cook it is in seawater. Yah?'

But all I could think of was *her*. Kiki. Kiki from the mountains in Northern Thailand, Dirk's companion at Ngam's, the outdoor restaurant where I'd taken my evening meals alone the previous summer. Kiki theatrically sucking her fingers and spitting bits of crab shells onto the red earth, next to where the mosquito coils burned and hissed, lacing the still evening air with their distinctive perfume.

Kiki and Dirk used to sit at the table next to the kitchen. And each evening, from my table tucked away in the far corner of the restaurant I'd observe them while pretending to write in my journal. Kiki, irreverent, animal-like in her beauty. Dirk, urbane and polished.

I could tell Kiki made the staff uncomfortable. She'd grunt her order without a please or thank you or any eye contact whatsoever. Dirk, on the other hand, was all charm and the waitresses fawned shamelessly over him. They'd beam as they passed by, carrying trays of food, trailing in their wake the sweet aromas of coconut milk and chilli-spiced sauce, and Dirk would grin up at them appreciatively and try to engage the better-looking waitresses in chat, while Kiki pouted. But when he'd eventually turn his chiselled face back on her, the two of them would giggle and eat from each other's plates like teenage lovers. The dynamics at their table intrigued me.

Thai music would sometimes blare from a small transistor radio, but mainly it was the sounds of nature; the gentle lapping of the nearby sea, the creaking and cracking of the forest trees, and the gabbing geckos, that accompanied our meals at Ngam's.

*

The first time I saw Kiki, I remember she was wearing shorts and a low-cut singlet. I was lying on the private beach, owned by Ngam's. It was the only beach in the vicinity safe for swimming. The morning mist hadn't yet lifted and the place was deserted. I'd already done my two-kilometre swim, and was starting a new book, when the pair of them rocked up, linking arms.

'Hello,' said Dirk and he flashed his tombstone teeth, dropped to his hunkers and asked what I was reading. It was the off-season and the resort was almost empty, so it was normal enough for westerners to gravitate towards each other.

Dirk said he was on a sabbatical from a university in Amsterdam. Kiki said nothing. Instead, she stared off into the distance, away from the beach and me. I tried to follow her gaze to see what she was so fascinated with but all I could see was a mass of green-clad trees that blurred into the horizon. She wasn't disposed to small talk or any talk, for that matter. And Dirk didn't introduce her.

Dirk and I became close. He had at least ten years on my nineteen and I was in awe of his worldliness. He was an expert on all things Thai.

I remember, I used to find the villagers' penchant for cockfighting unnerving. But he explained to me that they were normally such gentle folk, the aggression had to come out some way. Understanding people was his thing. All great literature is about people, he'd tell me. I suppose that seems obvious now, but back then everything he said seemed profound.

Sometimes too we'd go snorkelling and he'd point out the different rockfaces and sealife. And, sometimes, when the rains came, I'd while away the hours in their one-room cabin, chatting with Dirk and sipping tea or drinking beer, listening to the ropes of rain pounding the rooftop, while Kiki would observe us sulkily from their unmade bed, ostensibly painting her nails or plucking her eyebrows.

The last time I saw Kiki was when I called at their cabin to say goodbye. I had a rented Honda 250, and I always enjoyed the spin along the bumpy forest track out to their place. My mother had finally wired me money and I planned to fly on to Singapore. Dirk gave me a hug and wished me luck. Kiki offered me tea. The first time ever.

She looked me square in the face that afternoon, and I noticed her face was swollen, and her eyes puffy like she'd been crying. Dirk informed me offhandedly that he'd booked his flight home for one month's time. I presumed that was the reason for her foul humour. I wondered if she'd hoped for some sort of a long-term arrangement between the two of them, and I shook my head at her innocence. I declined the tea.

*

Dirk is in the middle of a monologue about his new apartment back in Amsterdam when our trendy waiter, speaking in a posh Dublin 4 accent, suggests a second bottle of wine. I nod to him to go ahead and open it. Dirk's new gaff is four hundred years old and still retains much of the original décor, apparently.

'Will we get the bill?' I interrupt. I don't care much for Dutch architecture, and I've had too much to drink to pretend.

I put up my arm and signal for the waiter. 'They're keen to close,' I say.

'Waiters are supposed to wait,' he says. He looks down at his lap and wipes his fingers vigorously on a napkin. 'That's what Kiki used to say. She hated being rushed.'

My cheeks colour. 'You still in touch with her?' I can't stop myself asking.

'Bitch,' he mutters. He crunches up his eyebrows and I startle, unsure for a moment if it's me or Kiki he's referring to. 'Hell no. She robbed me, took off with my passport and all my cash. I had to contact the embassy.'

'She was a prostitute?' I say. Somehow it seems important to clarify that detail.

'I wasn't paying her, if that's what you're implying. I respected her. Met her in Bangkok. Begged me to take her with me when she heard I was going south. Bangkok getting too rough, needed to get away from people, bad people, she said, and then of course I couldn't get rid of her.'

'Maybe she was desperate when she robbed you? I mean, you were leaving.'

'Tish,' he snorts and his whole face crumbles into an ugly contortion. 'They're survivors those girls, have to be.'

'Still,' I persist, 'you were with her how long? Eight months?'

'Ten,' he corrects. He taps his forehead, takes another slug of wine and lights up a cigarette without offering me one. 'I did see her again. Three weeks later, I'm waiting for the embassy to sort out a temporary passport. I go to say goodbye to friends, they live 40km away. Said they'd seen a girl who looked like Kiki. So, that evening, I go walking, down by the strip joints and cheap eateries. I wasn't expecting anything. There wasn't a lot going on. But then I see her, standing outside a run-down steel-shuttered club with two other girls. All three of them in high heels, covered in make up. I hardly recognise her. I cross the road. I'm mad as hell. I'm still waiting for my passport. I'm three days late for my new job at the university. She smiles, but then, all of a sudden, before I say anything she starts roaring. Some English blokes are drinking cans on the other side of the street. One of them calls over. "Is there a problem mate?" "He no pay," Kiki screams.

'And before I know it, I'm on the ground, they've emptied out my pockets, stolen my wallet and tossed it to Kiki. "Give the lady her money," a butty bloke covered in tattoos goes. "Fair is fair, these ladies gotta eat." Honour among scum, eh?' Dirk goes to pour himself more wine, but the bottle is already empty.

'I scramble to my feet. Kiki throws me a dirty grey smile. She'd been chewing betel, gone downhill a lot in the few weeks since I'd last seen her. Didn't look good.' He stubs out his cigarette on the glass ashtray and pulls a schoolboy face 'Thought she liked me. Two-faced slut.'

*

The sun has evaporated the bubbles off the bedroom window. It's turning into a bright day. I must have dozed off because it's already eleven-thirty. I toss on a shirt and squeeze into yesterday's jeans and am applying cheap face cream when the phone rings.

Intuitively, I know it's Dirk and perk up.

'Hi, didn't want to wake you earlier. You not working?'

'I've the morning off,' I say expectantly, even though I know he already knows.

'Think I leave my watch at your place. Be there in one half hour. We grab lunch. Yah?'

I scan the flat. Nothing. 'Have you tried the restaurant?' I say, thinking aloud. I spell out the name of last night's restaurant.

He thanks me. There's no further mention of lunch. It starts to rain outside.

I calculate my lost earnings. It's a Saturday, which would have meant double time, plus tips. I could do with the money.

Later, after my headache has eased, I go to change the bed sheets. A glimmer of metal catches my eye. I force my hand as far as it will go under the bedframe and I feel something cold. I yank out a watch.

'Waterproof at fifty metres. Worth at least three grand,' Dirk had boasted.

If I get a move on, I might catch him on his way out from the conference.

I go into the bathroom to do my make-up. My skin is pasty in the mottled mirror, my eyes puffy. I sit down on the toilet seat, and I imagine Dirk sitting in a lecture hall, surrounded by clever women, and any remnants of self-confidence I've left drain out of me.

And then, I think of Kiki, the uncouth prostitute from rural Thailand, and I feel a sudden kinship and I'm half-appalled.

I slip the outsized watch onto my narrow wrist.

Monday, I will take it to a jeweller's and get the bracelet reduced.

Encounter

Brian Kirk

Winter brings a shorter day,
a certain chill, a different light
that gives no heat to speak of.

I stop to breathe on ungloved hands,
a warmth that comes from inside
spreads while feet are freezing.

I must keep moving through the woods,
although the light is almost gone
and the way is rough. I must

watch out for tree roots, rocks; the moon
is draped in violet robes,
sun's legacy an afterglow

in the west. I see her standing
stock still on the path ahead,
crepuscular canine, red dog.

I stop and take her presence in;
those ears erect, black snout tip
dulled by clouds of icy breath.

She looks at me and holds me there –
I'm miles from home – her stillness
asks a question I can't answer.

And then she's gone, and I am
tramping on alone.

A Week Before the End the Swans Arrive

Sonya MacDonald

eight
make landfall
in the flooded field

November cakes my boots
the swans
glow white against the gloom

fires burn in every room
around the clock,
I lose the knack of sleeping

poised
      for
         flight

Trampoline

James Martyn Joyce

WITH MARY GONE TO HER sister's again Tom has the house to himself. Now he can have a proper look. The morning is fresh with the smell of recent rain, but the dull clouds have blown away to the east and the sun is out. He climbs the short ladder, dropping his slippers at the base, and crawls through the narrow opening into the meshed safety of the enclosure. Most of the rainwater has drained from the dark, rubberised membrane, but he can still feel the wet soaking through his socks. His grandson Shane has told him how you bounce way higher when the surface is wet. He lurches towards the centre.

'You're only old once.' He chuckles to himself.

A week earlier, Tom had been shaving when he heard the men's voices and the clinking of spanners through the open bathroom window. He was almost sure Mary had told him the delivery was that day, not that he was getting forgetful, no, there was just so much more to remember now, so many tedious, flitting intrusions. Chives, the next-door neighbours' annoying terrier, was spacing his barks evenly, a paced, delicate warning.

Tom squinted in the mirror, working the safety razor across his cheek, pulling the loose flesh of his neck this way and that, chasing the grey whiskers. He didn't get up as early anymore since the operation. He eased the saggy collar of his old T-shirt down to study the white line running from below his Adam's apple off into the mystery of grey chest hair.

How strange to dodge a bullet and still have a wound?

A shout from the garden and a drawn-out metal clatter. Tom stepped to the window and studied the scene below. An older workman was cutting into the lawn with a spade while a young helper tidied a jumble of metal bars and hooped tubing against the hedge. Chives' growls seeped through the greenery. That dog was a pest for sure.

Mary had first told him about the trampoline a few weeks earlier. How the grandchildren were bored when they visited and when she asked them, they said they'd love a trampoline. Tom held his tongue; they'd already commandeered both televisions: Shane stretched in front of the flatscreen killing camouflaged images to a background of crazed music, while Sally perched in the living area watching two girls barely older than herself demonstrating make-up routines on some YouTube channel.

By the time he'd had his breakfast the men were almost finished. They'd already clamped the rectangular base to the supporting legs and the younger man was busy checking the protective netting attached to the dark blue upright poles. The thing was bigger than Tom had expected and higher as well. It towered above the hedge and appeared even taller than his garden shed. The younger man crossed the sprung base in short, delicate hops, using his weight to gain height as needed.

'You won't catch me doing that,' Tom promised himself.

The very first time he'd ventured onto the dark surface Mary had gone to her sister's, like she did a few times a week. Tom vowed to stay on his knees. The bounce was almost too much for him even then, but in the end, he struggled upright, clinging to the safety netting. The Flannery-O'Briens, their next-door neighbours, were both at work, so he was safe enough. He could hear Chives snuffling along the hedge, worrying the wire mesh Tom had fitted to keep the little pest out.

Imagine even calling a terrier Chives?

He tried a few easy bounces, sticking close to the protective netting. He was amazed at the almost instantaneous loss of control, the dizzying urge to go higher, but he restrained himself. No sense in shattering a hip. Wasn't it funny how hips always shattered at his age, never snapped, and only rarely fractured?

In the afternoon he searched for trampolines on YouTube and just when he was picking up a lot of tips Mary texted him a shopping list. Going to the shops had become a bit of an ordeal. He would no sooner exit his front gate than Chives would be at his heels, nipping and growling, Tom trying to keep him away by swinging the empty shopping bag, the little fecker like a dervish. He blamed the Flannery-O'Briens; they'd discarded their own front gate soon after moving in.

'There are far too many barriers in the world already,' Fiona Flannery-O'Brien had explained to Mary.

Tom was on a learning curve just shy of vertical where the Flannery-O'Briens were concerned. They were youngish and soon after they'd moved in about nine months earlier, she'd told Mary that, for the future of the planet, they'd made a conscious decision not to have children. But, she confided, if she was ever to become pregnant, she'd be all in favour of a home birth.

'Does she do her own dental work as well?' had been Tom's reply.

The Flannery-O'Briens had rescued Chives from the local pound. He was the epicentre of their world.

They were also 're-wilding' their front and back gardens.

'We're returning the earth to its natural ecological condition,' was how Ciarán Flannery-O'Brien had put it while Tom was mowing his own mossy patch of front lawn.

Tom exited the house with his shopping bag and phone. He detoured to his shed to retrieve his secret weapon. The flat, plastic bottle nested among a variety of containers on the shelf just inside the door. The bottle held a weak mixture of disinfectant and water and it fitted snugly into his jacket pocket.

'Let the games begin,' he muttered as he reached the gate and Chives arrived at speed, like he'd been lying in wait, a growl building in his terrier chest as he closed on Tom's ankles. Tom swung the shopping bag and the dog veered away, trailing a throaty bark.

This battle continued until they reached the exit from the cul-de-sac and Tom turned right towards the shops. He rummaged in his pocket for the bottle. Chives was already slowing, but the dog still wasn't quick enough to avoid the thin stream of watery disinfectant which hit him squarely on the nose.

'Little fecker,' Tom muttered as Chives backed away, shook his head, and sneezed. These skirmishes had been happening for months, He felt the mutt might be learning, but it was a slow process.

Passing number fifty-eight, he waved to the figure behind the glass. He'd known Theresa Hannon since their schooldays, remembered kissing her on a summer's night in Salthill all those years ago. She was a widow now and she always smiled and chatted when they met.

He felt Mary mightn't like her.

The children loved the trampoline. Tom watched as they bounced and tumbled, turning somersaults at will, even floating higher than the roof of the garden shed, pointing towards the sea beyond the other houses.

While Mary, Sally and his daughter-in-law were shopping in town and his son was watching rugby on TV, Tom ventured on to the thing with Shane.

'Do it this way, granddad.' Shane kept his feet together and pushed into the black surface, bouncing higher and higher. Tom did as he was told, and it did help. He was getting better. Nowhere near as handy as Shane, but he managed to see over the garden hedge into the Flannery-O'Briens' backyard jungle.

'Re-wilding, my arse.' Tom muttered to himself.

When he drifted close to the safety netting Shane showed him how to push off again, using it to his advantage. After about ten minutes his chest bone began to hurt and he was sweating, so he eased off.

'Not a word to Dad or your granny.' He patted Shane on the shoulder. The child winked and touched a finger to his own lips.

On Tuesday evening, with the house quiet again, he was watching the weather forecast when he heard Ciarán Flannery-O'Brien talking to Mary at the front door. Probably something to do with Ciarán's plans to pressure the council into preserving the local green space to help save the bees, or the butterflies, or was it a rare slug? He went back to the weather woman on the TV.

'Tom, have you been teasing Chives?' Mary's question came out of nowhere. He muted the TV and explained how the dog attacked him every time he went to the shops.

'He's a little pest.'

'Ciarán says he smells of disinfectant. Someone told Fiona that you were squirting him with something from a bottle.'

'It was only water. Maybe there was a little disinfectant still left in there.' A white lie, the safety valve of most marriages. Then Mary went into the whole palaver of how they had to live here, how times were changing, how he couldn't just do as he pleased. Tom focused on the weather woman.

Mary didn't speak to him for the rest of the evening and went to her sister's earlier than usual the next morning.

Now he tries a tentative bounce, then another. The trampoline gives a rubberised sigh and throws him higher. He keeps his feet close together and pushes down into the wet surface, sails upwards. He's getting good at this.

He hits the surface harder, sees the top of the garden hedge below him. He hits the rubber mat again, higher still. Chives is lying asleep on the back doorstep, his head on his paws.

'Chi-i-ves!' He sings the dog's name as he sinks from view. He bounces again; the terrier is turning in a slow circle on the step. 'Chives!' he barks, sharp, staccato. The dog gives a tentative, confused yelp, spins faster as Tom descends. This time he pushes all his weight into the wet surface, bounces skywards once more, tries his first somersault, his shirt ballooning about him. 'Chiiiivvveees.' The mutt is spinning like a top now, coughing a crazed bark of canine confusion.

On Tom's next bounce the dog is slinking towards his kennel, his world scrambled, his head down. Tom tries a low, eerie ghost-whisper, 'Ch-i-i-i-v-e-s,' as the dog disappears inside. He feels there might be no further attacks. That balance has shifted.

And as he bounces, he marvels at all there is to see: a short ladder wedged behind the oil tank, almost buried in leaves. Is that his own ladder, which he's been missing for years and had presumed stolen? The stash of empty wine bottles snuggled by the chimney of May Doyle's extension where her son can't see them. And there's the guy renting number thirty-five, his shimmy as he crosses the fence into Kathleen Sullivan's neglected garden, his wife at work, her husband but an absent rumour.

And then there are the things he cannot see: how he will die at eighty-six, Mary gone before him. How his sons will post his death online with his favourite photograph of the three of them in the back garden, taken by Mary, pre-trampoline. Or Chives buried in the far corner beneath a carpet of re-wilded tangles after an unsuccessful skirmish with a Tesco delivery truck.

Nor can he see the Flannery-O'Briens moving out, the house sold, their marriage dissolved after Ciarán had impregnated a work colleague and they called the baby Dawn.

And he'll never see, or guess, how Theresa Hannon's heart flutters when he waves to her each day on his way to the shops. How her heart has skipped for all those years since that one bliss-filled night in Salthill. How he never, ever knew.

But for now, he bounces, the morning breeze through his billowing shirt, the wet chill of his socks forgotten, the caress of the autumn sun on his shoulders, his wispy hair awry, seeing beyond the hedge, beyond the other houses, each one with its own locked-in pain, but each one different, his gaze slipping past them all, all the way to the ocean.

The New Actaeon

Libby Maxey

Deer season stains the baited woods and makes
a trap of our familiar paths. The red
and orange, predatory or a plea
against the fate of prey, are sparks of fake
and jarring autumn. We take part. Instead
of watching warm September pull and ease
the maples' yellow through the canopy,
we look for hunters' perches warily,
imagining ourselves in sights. Twilight
and we have used up all the water where
a goddess might have bathed – no wonder, then,
our hounds now turn to us for blood. Our blight
is hoarding safety, sure our rightful share
is stasis – going out as we came in.

Storm

Kathy Miles

What shall I do with this wind, which gusts
with unrelenting force, its voice
an open mouth chanting a mantra of howl?

How do I stop the trees from breaking
their spines on this gale, patch up split trunks,
and glue the branches back again?

Rosebay grows dizzy with the endless sway;
spider tangled in threads of silk spins
round and round, a whirling carousel.

Leaves are grimly clutching to twigs,
but the clouds have escaped, skitter off
like loose slates, hurl themselves at a horizon

that lowers with the hammer-blow of squall.
Acorns are a crack on window-panes,
like the snap of broken bones.

What shall I do with this wind, which makes
the upright horizontal, sweeps legs and feet
from the ground, singing in its shrouds?

Ladybirds stagger through Mexican waves
of grass, foxgloves are Apache-dancing, throw
each other's stems in a tumult of passion.

I come to this weather with words burned
into me by August sun. Wind blusters away
the language of summer, leaves a hollow-out

like the empty oak on the crown of the hill
who speaks of his missing heartwood, threatens
to topple into himself, a blasted chimney.

What shall I do with this wind, but pocket it
in my coat-of-many-colours? Tumbles of late
butterflies, slow wither of last roses. I turn

back the hands of dandelion clocks. Each seed
a blowsy parachute, each seed an hour that's
flown, bringing me closer to the fractured dark.

Up the Glen

Deborah Moffatt

Later, in the bar, the mountain men drink
in cool camaraderie, in silence, in pain,
lips cracked, chapped, swollen,
eyes, wind-blind, weeping.
Elsewhere, upstairs
in the folds of a blanket,
in the unfolding pages of an atlas,
a storm rises.
Whatever they saw they keep to themselves:
an eternal emptiness of bare light
framing an elusive summit,
silver rock, ice.
For something as trivial
as lost sleep or loud laughter,
violence, unanticipated, shivers
through the glen.
Lives collide.
A mountain man, blind drunk,
might climb into that cold light
to lie in a strange bed.
A book falls, the binding broken,
pages torn, dark print sliding
over a frozen floor, words

disintegrating.
All through the night
the light rides the horizon,
behind the ridge, over a shoulder,
along the edge of a bed, never dimming.
In the morning everyone is a stranger,
sitting, eyes blurred, lips pursed,
in silence, in pain,
in cold hostility.

The Day Philip Larkin Died

Patrick Moran

That night, in the pub,
amid rituals
of spirit measures, draining glasses;
amid pool balls thudding,
the cards filling or failing;
amid the regulars'
hoary yarns, the gossip
retailed with edgy zest;
amid charged expletives
and muffled reveries;
in the cracks widening between
the said and the unsayable,
I sensed him somehow there,
sounding out the depths:
our costive souls
glimmering in his lines.

A Home Possessed

Jennifer McMahon

I'M HUNTING ALL OVER Dublin for a house, armed with auctioneers' brochures and internet search results, but a house is a cold shell of a thing, all straight lines and sharp edges. In chilling symmetry, walls face walls and floors face ceilings, as if they are being punished.

Stand in the corner, and face the wall. Don't move, until I tell ya.

Occupation gives a house purpose, and breathes life into its cold bones. Occupation gives it meaning. I'm not hunting a house. What I'm really looking for, like a hopeful stray scrabbling at the bars in a dog pound, is a *home*.

I say to the latest house:

Make me a part of you, and I will make you a part of me. We shall be one, you and me. People will say I live here with you, and they'll call me the lady who lives in that house. We'll possess each other, and you'll be a home possessed. Wouldn't that be a fine thing to wish for? Wouldn't that make your dreams come true?

The house doesn't want me though — it tells me in subtle ways, in shadows and reflections — and I'm not sure it's the one for me. I move on to the next, and the one after that, until the auctioneers are fed up with seeing me. Fussy bitch, I imagine them thinking. Time waster. Never satisfied, doesn't even know what she wants. Maybe they're right, but I'll know it when I see it.

*

Bad things happen in houses sometimes, and I've seen more than my fair share of them. Fathers get drunk, and beat mothers and children. Husbands get drunk, and beat their wives. All under a roof, supported by walls facing walls, with children turned to them because they spoke too loudly, or played too playfully.

Some fathers must be kind, I suppose, but I've yet to encounter their rare variety. Perhaps among my childhood friends, there were kind ones. If so, I was too timid to notice them. Timid was how they made me, and at home, it was how I was supposed to be. I carried it with me wherever I went, because it was easier than setting it down, then picking it back up again when I returned.

I had to get out, but my mother couldn't. Found a new home, with a husband who was my father with a different face, but with the same fists. Women marry their fathers, isn't that what they say? We weren't blessed with children, which was a blessing in itself. Again, I had to get out.

Such are the reasons, I want to tell the auctioneers, that I'm hunting not just a house, but rather a home. A place where no one is beaten, and I can play as playfully as I wish.

*

In October, I find the one I want, in a suburb shrouded by golden, atrophic leaves. The deal is done, and money changes hands, money that came to me through the sale of my father's house, after he finally passed away. The solicitor gives me the keys, and I go to my house and open the door. It has become more than it was. Now, it is a home possessed.

I dress it with softness, steep it in love, breathe life into its cold bones. Its colours are bright in the living room, soothing pastels in the trinity of bedrooms. The bath absorbs me, the lights illuminate me. I listen to the radio and sing along to the songs I like, even dance to them if it pleases me.

This is living, this is breathing. This is being home.

The neighbourhood assimilates me, and I fade into the background, become the lady who lives in that house. If they say anything else about me, it's only that I'm quiet, and keep myself to myself. I've enough of my own troubles to bear without being concerned for anyone else's, and the busiest person on the street is the one who minds their own business.

I make an occasional friend, and take the occasional lover. One is called Freddie. He's tall and thin, with icy hands that raise goosebumps on my flesh. He apologises for them, and blames his affliction on poor circulation. It has troubled him since childhood, and causes him great pain in the winter, when early frosts dress his car in white. I can't raise much sympathy for him, but I squeeze out an ounce of it in a tilt of my head, and a tight smile. We all have something to bear, I tell him, some torturous cross to carry. It's a crucifixion, he agrees, and I know what he means.

For a while, he's kind to me, and we carry our burdens side by side, then he fades away as if he were never really there at all. I erase his number, because it's unneeded, but I hold onto the memory of his hands. On frosty mornings, I think of him, and shiver. Cold hands, warm heart.

*

Regret is a beast with searing claws that tear my flesh, and pull me backwards until I am in another place, another time. I can't change the past, but I can relive it, even when I don't want to. I think of the lost years and what could have been done with them, had things been otherwise. I might have been someone else, if I hadn't been me and they hadn't been them, but things were exactly the way they were, and will forever remain so.

It's a frightening thing to be haunted by memory, but none of us are ever truly free of its grasp. My father lives in me, my husband too. The beast only ever sleeps lightly, and its wrath is easily drawn. Even in my sanctuary, their fists strike, their boots stomp. I stand and face the wall, because it's the only way to appease them.

See? I'm a good girl, not worthy of your attention.

To face a wall is to be an empty vessel. While I stand there, I do not exist. After a time, they subside, but I stay a while longer, just in case. It's not only my home that is possessed.

*

I function, and do the normal things. Shop for groceries at the local supermarket, cook, eat, sleep. My small front and back gardens are tidy. In the summer, I cut the grass, and sit out on the patio, absorbing light. Mostly, I'm alone. Sometimes, my brother Tommy visits.

Tommy is older than me, and has been battling cancer for three years. It will probably kill him, and I'm not surprised. As we sit and drink coffee in my bright kitchen, with the sun striping his face through the blinds, we talk about the venomous past. I think of how it sank its teeth into him, and pumped its poison deep within. The things we saw, the things we experienced, poisoned us both. In his case, it has twisted his guts into the tumours that are devouring him, even as we sit there.

For a moment, he waxes philosophical; the past is a nation with no flag, he tells me, and its anthem is a repetitive one. His expression turns to acid then, and he asks if we can ever be free of it, but I don't have an answer. Instead, I take his hand, to give him what comfort I may. It's a memento mori, as icy as Freddie's. Cold hands, warm heart. Cold, for his approaching death. Warm, for the life he still clings to.

When he leaves, when I close the front door and hear his car pull away, I put on some music, and dance to celebrate what remains of his time. It will not be long, I think.

*

Tommy dies in October, one year after I took possession of my house and made it my home. He was the last of my immediate family, and the bloodline ends with him. I think it's a good thing. The beast had to stop somewhere.

He's buried in a coffin, floor facing lid, walls facing walls, and him in the centre, forever turned to them as if he's being punished. Now, he's as cold as Freddie's hands, but we all turn to ice at the end. Maybe Freddie is already halfway there.

After the funeral, I sit in my kitchen, with the light streaking through the blinds, with tears in my eyes, and I talk to my father, wherever he is.

See what you made, Daddy? See what you broke?

It's the first time I've challenged him in such a fashion, and doing so makes me fearful; I've spoken too boldly. I stand and face the wall, to silence his replies.

Ya only got what ya deserved, and ya deserved no better.

Amen, amen, amen, over and over again. I pray as I did when I was a child, but they're nothing more than old and dusty doggerels, and I know that no one is listening. No god I'd ever want to believe in would allow a man to beat his wife in front of her own children, or beat children in front of their own mother. Still, I say the words, for the cold comfort they might bring.

Our father, who art wherever you are, let peace be upon this house, let peace be upon this home. May Tommy's soul, and all the souls of the Faithful Departed, rest in peace, if there really is such a thing.

*

The leaves yield to November's gales, and an early frost recalls Freddie and his malady to my mind. Stripped of their robes, I imagine the trees shiver like I did whenever he touched me. Snow comes, deepens, vanishes, then spring arrives, in foetal leaf buds and eager daffodils.

I surge with vitality, as do all living things in this season, while Tommy lies all alone in the cold ground. He is my memento mori, but also my memento habitas. I must live, and carry my memories with me. It's a crucifixion, just like Freddie said, but we all have our crosses to bear.

My home has become a haunted place. Again, I leave, because I must. When I close the door for the last time, it becomes a house again, a cold shell of a thing, all straight lines and sharp edges.

Floors face ceilings, walls face walls, as if they are being punished.

Stand in the corner, and face the wall. Don't move, until I tell ya.

Mirror

Jan Mordenski

Clearly she's nothing without you,
a transparent bit of glass, quicksilver,
a flat monotonous figure who's,
truthfully, found herself up against
a wall most of her life. Face it,
without you, she draws a blank,
comes up empty in the middle,
a five of diamonds without the centre
jewel. At night she's perfectly useless,
staring into the oncoming day
with nothing on her mind, not even
a glimmer of thought running across
her passive, pale face. It's a time like that
you'll come to her, turn on all the lights,
spend a few moments in quiet reflection,
only to see it's your own face she's taken on,
again, talking back to you in your own words,
in the vague modulations of your own voice.

City in October in the Rain

Luke Power

Cars surge through the night, the nightlife,
urban ships setting out into open water,
tyres leaving a rippling wave in their wake.
There is more than just muck, more than road-water:
see the yellow streetlamps, headlight flash and stars
all rushing over the shoes of a young woman, a man –
and from that wave a ripple further
of swears and curses and then laughter pealing off
down side streets, badly lit but for the glow
of cigarettes caught in conversation, like fireflies,
like stars. And did I mention the rain?

It spreads the canvas for this cold Saturday
in soft sheets, coursing – and suddenly there's poetry,
and people huddle together under wind-whipped umbrellas,
the young man in love or just a loving young man
throwing his jacket across his companion, streetlamp yellow,
their steps unsteady from wine and shared laughter.
Older souls – knowing better – wait it out, hold the line,
those stooped streetlights and spectres watching time disappear
across cobbles, moving on down towards the sea, the pier,
and still it falls, painting this city or perhaps revealing it,
the raindrops restless and maddening and wonderful.

I'm moving through the downpour now and moved by it,
feeling beneath the noise and anxieties which breed and gain interest
that there is a kind of peace settling at the bottom of myself,
a yellow glow, a whispering flame,
a wondering which hasn't yet got a name.
And while those moths who gather round flickering heaters
lose themselves in the night and in their youth,
I keep on through the rain, the city murmuring its songs
to the listener, the watcher, the mute.

Returning to the Garden

Charles Wilkinson

as if present in the breeze, lifting the latch

so mother comes back as a ghost –
a glide through the gate to her garden

    a shiver of white butterflies,
    is how wings vibrate
    as though from another side

& now
    light is
      at variance:
cloud-thinned, & eking
out the colours of plants
lengthened into the eye
as though inside there
    & all ready

a shift in wind speed
brings a blue-gapped sky:
the consequent reshuffle
of shadow over flower-
beds, ruined into weeds,

their liveries of wildness:
      spurge & bluebell
        couch grass, groundsel
        speedwell, yarrow;

  on the verge, by the box hedge,
   raceme of golden rods,
late summer sustenance for bees

& some days, what her hands planted –
peonies, primulas & starfire phlox

Migrations

Susan Isla Tepper

First, nobody helped

After the garden apartment fire I learned about birds. Dragging all her burnt belongings to the dumpster. Watching the migrations circling and clacking. A black sky and very cold. Almost Christmastime. Mom's neighbour admonishing me to wear a jacket. Sum total of the help we received. I couldn't be bothered with jackets. Way too much to clean up. Her sooty walls smudged like the night sky. Bedsheets lost in the blaze. We pushed together two twin beds and slept under a designer throw. This is a boutique town. Nobody sells bedsheets. Or pillow cases. We slept with the mattresses bare beneath us. Me and Mom. So skeletal after her ordeal. I just kept cleaning things. The insurance company took her clothes away. Half a week later the clothes were returned. Mom and I ecstatic. Hanging up her freshly cleaned clothes. Then I noticed a fire smell. Pulling her clothes back down off the hangers. All that time wasted tearing those paper twisty things from the clothing tags. Mom keeping up a good front. Boxes piled high in her living room. Those we piled outside could almost touch the migrations.

Second, I told everyone

People I'd never met before heard the fire story. I told everyone. Couldn't help it. At CVS, Walgreens, Dunkin Donuts, Stop & Shop, the pizza place, hardware store, the laundromat. Most of our provisions came from CVS. It was the closest. Eggs, milk, bread, butter, chips, soups, toothpaste, soap, detergents, paper products. The boy at the register in CVS told me his own story. About his younger brother dying last year. The boy was brave and sorrowful. It quelled my own fears. The ladies running the laundromat gave me change and sort of listened. Their hard lives etched on their faces. I cried the moment I stepped in there and heard the washing machines sloshing. Washing Mom's still smoky clothes and sheets and towels. I cried every day in there. Someone asked me why don't you use wash & fold. I saw the clothes sometimes dropped on the floor during wash & fold. There's a type of moat along the front of the washers. It fills with dirty water. I've seen clothes land in the moat. Then they are dried and folded.

Third, all that was porous

It became a matter of moving things. Back and forth, room to room. Nothing seemed to lighten or change much. I filled the car trunk with smoked clothes. When that was jammed I filled the interior. Working my way through the car every day. Some things never become free of smoke. Two washings and it was history. Each pair of pants or top or dress had its own history. Mine was unravelling with the passage of time. I remembered her in the royal blue crepe at my cousin's daughter's wedding. Mom. Skeletal angel. We kept our hygiene separate. I couldn't take the risk of getting sick. Then what. I washed up in the kitchen sink each morning. Afterwards scouring it with Ajax. Mom always hovering like the frail beach birds she loves. We had to throw away all that was porous. Her old wooden rolling pin. Over the years it rolled out crusts for thousands of pies. Apple, peach, chocolate cream, lemon meringue, pumpkin. She hated parting with it. Held it a moment like you hold a baby. Said it belonged to her mother. Said oh well. Handing it over to me. I sank.

Fourth, evacuation

The apartment management agreed to paint. But it will cost you they said. Mom lived here twenty years. Moved here when Dad died. Never had a paint job. No matter. Cash only. We'll need you to evacuate a few hours one of them said. I left cash in an envelope on the glass coffee table. Drove the two of us to her little bay beach. We laughed about the load of smoky clothes in the back seat. Slowed down at the house with the mullioned porch windows. Dad's grown-up brother and his wife had rented it every summer. Dad and his brothers got one glorious week out of the tenement. We sat there looking at the house. I imagined Dad poised on the gravel driveway. The first out to go for a morning swim. I got out of the car and touched the cement wall. Old and cracked. Where he may have lingered. Then we drove into the deserted beach area. Parked and watched the grey swells. The gulls. The tiny birds with skinny legs. The long pier empty of people. Small waves hitting up and down the beach. Masts of moored boats clanking. We talked about other things. Anything. Funny things when we kids were growing up. My dad. Sooner or later it always harkened back to him. She said You are your father's daughter. I knew what she meant. How he'd get it all pulled together.

The Crannóg Questionnaire

Ron D'Alena

How would you introduce yourself as a writer to those who may not know you?

I'll be honest, I didn't make a living as a writer, so I don't yet have the backbone to introduce myself as a writer. In a social setting, when asked the question 'So, what do you do?', my initial response is that I'm retired from the tech industry. Usually someone will follow up with 'So how do you spend your time now?' and I'll give them a list of stuff I enjoy doing, which includes writing. This is the point when, if the person is interested, I'll talk about my writing.

When did you start writing?

When I was around ten, I took an end-table and the volume of *Encyclopaedia Britannica* dealing with the wild west into our garage and asked my family not to disturb me because I would be busy writing a western. I think I wrote three sentences before getting hungry and abandoning the project for a hot dog. In high school I wrote and submitted a few stories to a fantasy-sword-and-sorcery publication. They were rejected with a note telling me to send more, which I didn't. And in college I was lucky enough to have a piece of fiction published in the school journal. And for decades that was the end of my frivolous writing.

In my professional life, as part of my job, I wrote custom market analysis reports, white papers and syndicated research/analysis reports pertaining to the high technology industry. Years after I left the tech industry and moved from California to Oregon, I began writing fiction in earnest. That was around 2010.

Do you have a writing routine?

In the morning, after a bunch of coffee and letting the dogs out to do their business, I write for three or so hours. Throughout the day I'll return and write a bit more. At the end of the day, I'll write some more and wordsmith and think through the next morning's writing.

When you write, do you picture somehow a potential audience or do you just write?

With respect to my short story collection, I was thinking more along the lines of the *type* of story than I was about a particular audience. I knew the stories would eventually be gathered into a collection, so writing each story in a similar voice and style was important. That said, I thought these stories would appeal to a particular audience, readers who want a literary style and are looking for stories about ordinary people and plausible situations. My philosophy for this project was: *if I build it, they will come.*

Now I've switched gears. I'm currently writing a crime thriller novel. Understanding the expectations of the potential audience for this genre is a key consideration. With this project, I'm writing for the reader, not myself.

Some writers describe themselves as planners, while others plunge right in to the writing. Would you consider yourself a planner or a plunger?

I'm a planner. I have a writing process, unquestionably stemming from grunting through graduate school papers and work reports. My process is very analytical. It includes outlining/bullet-pointing main ideas and compartmentalising different sections (of a short story) or chapters (for a novel).

I begin writing in earnest after I have a solid idea of how the story plays out – from beginning to end. Ok, so I start writing and things change: names, motivation, atmosphere, plot, et cetera. At the beginning of the outlining process, I know this will happen, that things will change and change again. But I can't begin a story unless I've gone through my analytical routine.

I'm also a big rewriter as I'm moving along. Yes, my writing friends tell me this is a big no-no. Just get the whole damn thing on paper before editing, they tell me. But I like polishing as I carve. Seeing a polished sentence motivates me. My style of writing requires the correct word in the correct spot. At the end of the process my draft is tight. Now it's time to rewrite. Rewrite. Polish. Polish.

All in all, I'm a slow, methodical writer.

How important are names to you in your books? Do you choose the names based on liking the way they sound or for the meaning? Do you have any name-choosing resources you recommend?

Name selection is very important during the writing process. Yes, often I'll select something based on how it sounds or its meaning. That said, when I first dole out a name, I'm sure it'll change as I move along and better understand the character and the story.

Here are a few examples from *The Madness of Being* of selecting names to fit a character:

1) I needed a tough name to fit the main guy in *Polka Dots*. I used the name *Buell*. Got it from Buell Motorcycles. 'Buell, standing in the middle of the kitchen, opened his beer, guzzled it down.'

2) In *Plastic Box* I needed a name that fit an elderly woman. 'Eleanor was reaching for the restaurant door handle when she caught sight of her arthritic knuckles and the array of age spots across the back of her hand.'

I'll give you two more examples of naming. This one involves naming a street. In *Bonnie, Troy and Tommie* we have a woman who just received a foreclosure notification. Bonnie's life is falling apart. I placed her on *Haven Street*. Haven meaning a place of refuge, which is the opposite of her situation. 'She knew her life on Haven Street was over, done with. Strangers in banks and politicians were telling her to start something new.' Secondly, *Bonnie* means *pretty* – a *bonnie lass*. But my Bonnie is frazzled and addicted to prescription drugs. Again, the opposite of her reality. My description of her is: 'Bonnie stood there, wrapped in cigarette smoke and loneliness. She was tired.'

Name-choosing resources ... well ... I begin by looking online at baby naming sites. Often this does the job. But there are times when the correct name can't be found in this manner. At this point, the hunt begins, everything is fair game. I become aware of billboards and signs and labels. I got Wade's last name, *Nickles*, from an insurance billboard; the insurance guy's last name was Nickles. I got Jim's name from looking at a bottle of Jim Beam behind the bartender. Et cetera.

Is there a certain type of scene that's harder for you to write than others? Love? Action? Erotic?

I approach every type of scene in the same manner. I begin by stepping back as if I were a reporter and bullet point the scene components. Then I dive down and lose myself in the writing. I'll add that I haven't and don't expect to write erotic. At this point it's just not my gig.

An example of a love scene (from *The Madness of Being*):

'There was a moment of tenseness then Mike leaned into her, used his forefinger to wipe the perspiration from her left cheek. She let him kiss her lips. Surrounded by the twilight, they kissed hard. Her smell made him lightheaded. He slid his forefinger under her right tank top strap and made little caressing circles upon her collarbone then he untwisted the thin shoulder strap of her tank top, damp and clingy from humidity. *How many years has it been since I felt her kiss? Over fifteen. Damn, how did I let that happen? Why did I let that happen? What's wrong with me?*'

— *The Accident*

An example of an action scene (from *The Madness of Being*):

'As soon as Joyce hit the ground, Alice scrambled over and used the tip of her right shoe to roll the prostrate woman into the pool.

"Oh, shit!" Ruth whispered, looking at Alice in astonishment.

Joyce was motionless as she sank, face down, arms stretched out, legs spread-eagled. Bubbles streamed up from around her silver fox hair. Then the bubbles stopped, and she rose slowly to the surface. When she broke water level, the two women looked at each other as the floating body nudged gently against the poolside.'

— *Extra Weight*

Tell us a bit about your non-literary work experience, please.

My professional career started and ended in Silicon Valley. After receiving a BS in Business Administration (Finance) and a BA in Economics, I worked for a few market research/consulting companies, and expanded my responsibilities from market analyst to developing contracts for customised consulting projects. I then took time away from work and earned a master's degree in Business Administration (Finance). Afterwards I worked for an international bank in the technology market research department. And ended that portion of my life in a networking company where I held various jobs in project and people management.

What do you like to read in your free time?

I mostly read fiction, interspersed with nonfiction, guitar magazines and fishing magazines. I don't read writing journals—maybe I should. I read most every night. I'd like to give a shout out to a memoir I just read by Dan Branch called *Someday I'll Miss This Place Too*. It's about Dan's experience as a novice lawyer in a remote Alaskan town. Poignant. Well worth the read. Highly recommended.

What one book do you wish you had written?

The Grapes of Wrath. Some honourable mentions include *The Good Earth*, *To Kill A Mockingbird* and *Where the Red Fern Grows*.

Do you see writing short stories as practice for writing novels?

Yes, writing short stories, for me, has been a practice ground for a novel project. The experience has allowed me to develop my writing voice. And seeing many of these stories published in quality journals/magazines has given me the confidence to step up my game.

Do you think writers have a social role to play in society or is their role solely artistic?

I think writers should write what they want to write.

My short stories are riddled with social commentary. My characters are confronted with domestic violence, prescription drug abuse, family strife, financial difficulties, illness, aging and infidelity. I also strive for aesthetics in my writing style, for a voice where beauty, brevity and honesty reside within sentences whenever possible. Writers can wear both hats simultaneously: one social, the other artistic.

Tell us something about your latest publication, please.

My latest publication is *The Madness of Being*, a collection of fifteen short stories. Thirteen stories have been previously published, while two stories were written specifically for the collection. Also, two of the stories were nominated for the Pushcart Prize. An excerpt from Tammy Ruggles's book review for *Readers' Favorite* states 'If you like edgy stories about the ordinary or life's "underbelly", you will love *The Madness of Being*.'

I think I like Tammy's quote.

Can writing be taught?

Writing *is* taught. University students receive writing degrees every year. In a less formal setting, there are seminars and magazines and books and videos and groups that help/teach people how to write. So, yes, you can be taught the mechanics of telling a story – stuff like constructing a setting, character development, plotting, POV, et cetera. I also think that writing students walk away with confidence in their writing. Why? Well, because their work has been tested and commented on by their peers and teachers. Confidence goes a long way when submitting work to prospective publishers.

However, great writing transcends rules and mechanics. Writing a great story is a creative endeavour, and creativity is difficult to teach. Some people are natural storytellers – no formal training required. It's in their blood. Besides a healthy dose of innate creativity, I believe a storyteller is helped by life experiences, good listening and observational skills, persistence and the ability to accept constructive advice.

Do I think a formal writing education is necessary to produce good writing? No.

Have you given or attended creative writing workshops and if you have, share your experiences a bit, please.

No, I've never given any writing workshops. I have attended a workshop. I was eighteen, my mom pointed me in the direction of a Saturday creative writing workshop at a local college. One of the exercises had us writing for half an hour while ambient music played. I thought that was pretty cool. To this day, I have music playing while engaged in a project. During the brainstorm/whiteboard/outline stage, I listen to an array of music: blues, jazz, Afro-Cuban, progressive, fusion, most anything. However, when I get down and dirty into the actual writing, I've got ambient, soft instrumental or classical going.

Finally, what question do you wish that someone would ask about your writing, and how would you answer it?

Most people when discussing the subject first ask:

'Have you ever been published?';

followed by: 'You make any money from it?';

followed by: 'What genre do you write?'

It would be cool if they'd asked: 'Why do you write?'

After which I'd explain that I'm compelled to write, or at least to think about writing. Writing for me is like piecing together a mammoth puzzle. It's problem-solving. It's great fun. And when the puzzle is completed to the best of my ability, I get a great deal of satisfaction.

Artist's Statement

Cover image: *Red Forest*, by Jean Rooney

Jean Rooney is an Irish artist currently living and working on unceded and unsurrendered Wolastoqey Territory in New Brunswick, Turtle Island. She is a graduate of the National College of Art and Design, Ireland. For over twenty years, she has exhibited and worked internationally as a professional artist. In the last ten years, she has worked with 4,000 students through 19 artist residencies on collaborative art projects in Canada. She is Head of Graduate Studies – Advanced Studio Practice at the New Brunswick College of Craft and Design, Eastern Canada. She is also a PhD student in the Faculty of Fine Arts at Concordia University, Montreal, Québec.

Biographical Details

Deborah Bacharach is the author of two full-length poetry collections, *Shake & Tremor* (Grayson Books, 2021) and *After I Stop Lying* (Cherry Grove Collections, 2015). Her poems, book reviews and essays have been published in *Crannóg*, *Poetry Ireland Review*, *New Letters* and *Poet Lore* among many others. DeborahBacharach. com.

Byron Beynon coordinated Wales's contribution to the anthology *Fifty Strong* (Heinemann). His work has featured in several publications including *Agenda*, *Black Fox Literary Magazine*, *Wasafiri*, *Cyphers*, *The London Magazine*, *Poetry Wales*, *English: Journal of the English Association*, and the human rights anthology *In Protest* (University of London and Keats House Poets). He has published several collections, including *The Echoing Coastline* (Agenda) and *Where Shadows Stir* (The Seventh Quarry Press).

Annette C. Boehm is the author of *The Apidictor Tapes* (April 2022) and *The Knowledge Weapon*. She serves as a poetry reader for *Memorious* and has also authored two intertextual chapbooks available from Dancing Girl Press. Annette cboehm.wordpress.com

David Butler's novel *City of Dis* (New Island) was shortlisted for the Kerry Group Irish Novel of the Year, 2015. Arlen House published his second short story collection, *Fugitive*, in 2021.

Siobhan Campbell was awarded the Listowel Writers' Week Irish Poem of the Year in 2021. Her latest work appears in the anthologies *Vital Signs*, *100 Poems to Save the Planet*, and *An Empty House: Poetry and prose on the climate crisis*.

Enda Coyle-Greene's first collection, *Snow Negatives* won the Patrick Kavanagh Award in 2006 and was published by the Dedalus Press in 2007. Her subsequent collections are *Map of the Last* (2013) and *Indigo, Electric, Baby* (2020), both also from Dedalus. Co-founder and Artistic Director of the Fingal Poetry Festival, she received a Patrick and Katherine Kavanagh Fellowship in 2020.

Emily Cullen is the Meskell UL-Fifty Poet in Residence. Her third collection, *Conditional Perfect* (Doire Press, 2019), was included in *The Irish Times* round-up of the best new poetry of 2019. She is also a harper and a former Director of Cúirt International Festival of Literature and the Patrick Kavanagh Centenary.

Phil Cummins is a Dublin-born academic and writer now living in County Kildare. His short stories and essays have featured in various anthologies and literary magazines. His writing achievements include honourable mention (2020) and shortlist (2022) for the Fish Memoir Prize.

Barbara De Franceschi has published four collections of poetry and her work has appeared in many anthologies, newspapers and journals Australia-wide, online and in other countries.

Maurice Devitt is a past winner of the Trocaire/Poetry Ireland and Poems for Patience competitions, he published his debut collection, *Growing Up in Colour*, with Doire Press in 2018. Curator of the Irish Centre for Poetry Studies site, his Pushcart-nominated poem *The Lion Tamer Dreams of Office Work* was the title poem of an anthology published by Hibernian Writers in 2015.

Clive Donovan is the author of two poetry collections, *The Taste of Glass* (Cinnamon Press) and *Wound Up With Love* (Lapwing) and is published in a wide variety of magazines including *Acumen, Agenda, Crannóg, Prole, Sentinel* and *Stand*. He lives in Totnes, Devon, UK. He is a Pushcart and Forward Prize nominee for 2022's best individual poems.

Billy Fenton lives in Tramore. His work has been published widely including in *The Rialto, New Irish Writing, The North, Crannóg, Abridged,* and *Orbis*.

Cian Ferriter's first published poem appeared in *Crannóg*. Since then he has won the 2019 Westival International Poetry Competition, was a runner-up in the 2020 Gregory O'Donoghue International Poetry Prize and was highly commended in the 2021 Troubadour International Poetry Prize. His debut chapbook *Earth's Black Chute* won the 2022 Munster Fools for Poetry Competition and was published by Southword in May 2022.

Joel Fishbane's novel *The Thunder of Giants* is available from St Martin's Press.

Lisa Frank received her MFA in Creative Writing from Eastern Washington University and has published fiction, poetry, creative non-fiction and screenplays. In 2016 she won second place in the Francis MacManus Short Story Competition and in both 2015 and 2020 she was a joint-winner of the Irish Writers' Centre Novel Fair Competition. Co-director of Doire Press, she is also the editor of *Galway Stories* and co-editor of *Belfast Stories* and *Galway Stories: 2020*.

Bernadette Gallagher is a widely published poet. She received an Arts Council Agility Award in 2021. Bernadettegallagher.blogspot.ie

Shauna Gilligan is a novelist and short story writer. Her fiction has been widely published including in *Crannóg*, and she has received awards for her writing including a Creative Ireland Arts Act Grant (Kildare Co. Co.). Her latest publication is *Mantles* (Arlen House, 2021), a collaboration with visual artist Margo McNulty.

Kevin Graham's poems have appeared in various magazines and newspapers. His first collection is due out in 2023.

Richard W. Halperin's poetry collections are published by Salmon and by Lapwing. In autumn 2023 Salmon will bring out a selected and new volume, drawing upon his twenty previous collections and including 25+ new poems.

Joanne Hayden is a writer and arts journalist. Her fiction has been shortlisted for the Francis MacManus award and published in journals including *Crannóg*, *Ambit*, *Banshee*, *York Literary Review* and *Splonk*. Her play *Salvage* was shortlisted for the 2021 Fishamble/ESB Tiny Plays for a Brighter Future award.

Ann Howells edited *Illya's Honey* for eighteen years. Her recent books are: *So Long As We Speak Their Names* (Kelsay Press, 2019) and *Painting the Pinwheel Sky* (Assure Press, 2020). Two of her four chapbooks were published through contests: *Black Crow in Flight* (Main Street Rag Publishing, 2007) and *Softly Beating Wings* (Blackbead Books, 2017). Her poems appear in small press and university journals.

Monica Igoe has worked for a number of years as a journalist in London, Cork, Dublin and Galway. This is her first short story.

Maria Isakova Bennett works as a tutor for charities and creates the hand-stitched poetry journal *Coast to Coast to Coast*. Her awards include The Poetry Society's Peggy Poole, 2020, and a Northern Writers' Award. She has created collaborative work with over 100 poets from the UK, Ireland, and France. With poet John Glenday she created *mira* (an exhibition and journal, 2020). She has published five pamphlets of poetry, the latest is *Painting the Mersey in 17 Canvases* (Hazel Press, 2022)

Brian Kirk has published a poetry collection, *After The Fall* (Salmon Poetry, 2017) and a short fiction chapbook, *It's Not Me, It's You* (Southword Editions, 2019). His poem *Birthday* won Irish Book Awards Poem of the Year, 2018. He was a winner of the Irish Writers Centre Novel Fair 2022 with his novel *Riverrun*. www.briankirkwriter.com.

Sonya MacDonald has been published in *Mslexia*, *Northwords Now*, the *Eildon Tree*, *Causeway/Cabhsair*, and was chosen to feature in an anthology of work celebrating the centenary of the artist Joan Eardley. *All Becomes Art (Part 1)* was published by Speculative Books in 2022.

Jennifer McMahon's work appears in the *Oxford Prize Anthology* and *Solstice Literary Journal*. She won the Bray Literary Festival flash fiction competition 2022. She was a Top Ten Finalist in the Oxford Prize (Summer 2022), and her short stories have been shortlisted for the Anthology Short Story Award, the Alpine Fellowship Writing Prize, the Wild Atlantic Writing Awards, and the Women On Writing Flash Fiction Prize. She was also shortlisted for The Literary Consultancy Scholarship in 2022. Her novel *House Devil* was longlisted for Fiction Factory's Novel First Chapter competition. Her genre stories have twice appeared in *Frontier Tales*.

James Martyn Joyce lives and writes in Galway.

Libby Maxey is a senior editor at the online journal Literary Mama. Her work has appeared in *Emrys* and *The Maynard*, among others, and her chapbook *Kairos*

(2019) won Finishing Line Press's New Women's Voices Contest. She is also a winner of the 2021 Princemere Poetry Prize.

Kathy Miles's work has appeared widely in magazines and anthologies. Her fourth full collection of poetry, *Bone House*, was published by Indigo Dreams in 2020.

Deborah Moffatt has published three collections of poetry, *Eating Thistles* (Smokestack Books, 2019) and *Far From Home* (Lapwing, 2004) in English, and *Dàin nan Dùil* (Clàr, 2019) in Scottish Gaelic. A fourth collection, in Gaelic, is forthcoming from Clàr. Her work in English has appeared most recently in *Poetry Salzburg Review*, *Shearsman* and *Poetry Scotland*.

Patrick Moran has published four collections of poetry, the most recent being *Reckonings* (Salmon, 2019). His poems have appeared widely in Irish outlets; and also in the UK.

Jan Mordenski is a teacher and trained folklorist from Metro Detroit. She has been published in the US in such journals as *Arete, Hamilton Stone Review, Plainsong* and *The MacGuffin* and her poem *Crochet* was selected by Ted Kooser for inclusion in the online series American Life in Poetry. In Ireland she has had work published by Salmon Poetry, The Connacht Tribune, and Treoir.

Luke Power has been published in *New Irish Writing, ROPES, Sonder* and others. He is working on a novel.

Ana Reisens was the recipient of the 2020 Barbara Mandigo Kelly Peace Poetry Award. She has been published in *Channel, The Mud Season Review*, and *The Bombay Literary Magazine*, among others.

Stephen Shields's work has been published in *Poetry Ireland Review, The Stony Thursday Book, AGENDA, The SHOp*, and previously in *Crannóg*, among others.

Morag Smith has been widely published in magazines and anthologies including *Poetry Ireland Review* and *Gutter*. Her first pamphlet, *Background Noises,* which was inspired by a semi-derelict psychiatric hospital in Renfrewshire, was launched by Red Squirrel Press in November 2022.

Susan Isla Tepper's stage play *The Crooked Heart*, a ficitonalised account of artist Jackson Pollock in his later years, had a staged-reading at The Irish Rep Theatre, NYC, on October 25th, 2022. She has received many honours and awards for her writing.

Laura Treacy Bentley's work has been widely published in the United States and Ireland in *The New York Quarterly, Art Times, The Southern Poetry Anthology, Poetry Ireland Review, The Stinging Fly, Crannóg*, and it was featured on *A Prairie Home Companion, Poetry Daily, O Magazine*, and *Publishers Weekly*. She is the author of *Looking for Ireland: An Irish Appalachian Pilgrimage*; a psychological thriller set in Ireland, *The Silver Tattoo*; a short story prequel, *Night Terrors*; a poetry collection, *Lake Effect*; and her first picture book, *Sir Grace and the Big Blizzard.*

Jean Tuomey is published in national and international journals. Her chapbook *Magical Thinking* was highly commended in Fools for Poetry 2021. Her first poetry collection, *Swept Back* (Lapwing), was published in 2022. A former teacher, she trained as a writing facilitator with the National Association for Poetry Therapy in the US.

Charles Wilkinson's poetry collections include *The Snowman and Other Poems* (Iron Press), the pamphlet *Ag & Au* (Flarestack) and *The Glazier's Choice* (Eyewear), Website: http://charleswilkinsonauthor.com

Landa Wo's poetry has appeared in a variety of publications including *Bellingham Review, Michigan Quarterly Review, Nashville Review, Poetry New Zealand, Raleigh Review, Salt Hill Journal, Spillway, Tule Review, The Common, The Cape Rock*, and several anthologies. He is an Afro-French poet and member of Société des Poètes Français. @wo_landa.

Stay in touch with
Crannóg
@
www.crannogmagazine.com